Encountering Church

David R Peel

With contributions from

Jill Thornton

and

Alan Gaunt

The United Reformed Church

The
United
Reformed
Church

Encountering Church
David R Peel

ISBN 0 85346 257 7

Published by The United Reformed Church
86 Tavistock Place, London WC1H 9RT

Produced by Communications and Editorial, Graphics Office.

CONTENTS

**For my friends and colleagues
in the United Reformed Church**

PREFACE

This book contains a series of addresses and sermons which I delivered during 2003-6, mostly when I was Moderator of the General Assembly of the United Reformed Church (2005-6). They form a sustained enquiry about the future of the Christian church at a period when mainstream churches are facing a deep crisis. While they were written primarily for the United Reformed Church a great deal of what I say has wider ecumenical relevance.

Part One raises some of the issues we now face as a church. Chapter One contains an address which was originally given to the Mersey Synod in November 2003 in which I asked the question: Has the United Reformed Church got a future? and concluded that, in its present configuration, neither it nor its congregations have much life left! Then I explore the need for the church to present and live the gospel in ways which are liberated from contemporary church culture. Chapter Two originated in a sermon first delivered in Aysgarth Parish church.

Part Two represents an attempt to address today's big ecclesial issues. Chapter Three contains my Moderator's Address which was delivered to the General Assembly on the 2nd July 2005. The framework for an encountering church which I outlined at Warwick University is followed by the theme talks I gave to last year's Holiday Forum based on Acts 2: 42 Chapter Four argues that the church has three core activities from which the whole of its life flows. Learning, fellowship and worship thus become the springboard for the church's mission. Chapter Five contains the St Columba's lecture which I gave in Oxford on the 31st October 2005. Its central idea it is then developed in Chapter Six on 'pendulum theology', while Chapter Seven, which began life as a sermon delivered in the Westminster College, Cambridge chapel, is a plea to regain an imaginative approach to the Bible that respects its literary genre. Chapter Eight in Part Three contains my concluding reflections as Assembly Moderator.

A great deal of this material has been 'peddled' around the United Reformed Church on my travels as its Moderator. Its development reflects the many interesting and challenging comments I have received. For these, and all the support I have received while carrying out my duties, I am very grateful. Jill Thornton's leadership of worship at Assembly and Mission Council will be remembered long after my words. I owe her a profound debt. My Chaplain's words and presence, thoughtfulness and common sense have been greatly appreciated. I am pleased that some of the material she created is contained in this book. Alan Gaunt, was once my minister in Keighley. He has contributed a hymn based upon the readings which have stimulated so much of my recent theology. To him and to Jill I offer my thanks for allowing their work to grace this book.

My wife prepared the manuscript for publication under a great deal of pressure. Her support, and that of the rest of my family, has been a source of unending encouragement as I regained strength after a serious illness. Nothing in my life would make much sense without Pat, with whom I shared my memorable Moderatorial journeys.

David R Peel
Durham
27th April 2006

PART ONE

ISSUES AND CHALLENGES

PRAYER OF ADORATION AND CONFESSION

Living God,
as I look out from a mountain top
and consider the vastness of the creation below me,
as I look closely at a spider's web
and consider the intricacy of the creation around me,
as I look up to the stars in the heavens
and consider the mystery of the creation above me,
I catch my breath, in wonder and in awe,
and ask for your forgiveness
for the times when I think I can define you.

Living God,
when I hold a new born child in my arms
and consider the miracle of life,
when I see your pain in the eyes of another
and consider the depths to which you will go to stand alongside us,
when I am held in the arms of someone I love
and consider the miracle of human love,
I catch my breath, in wonder and awe,
and ask for your forgiveness
for the times when I think I can limit you.

Living God,
as I feel my pulse race in the midst of debate
and consider the many ways you inspire me,
when I feel the hairs on the back of my neck rise
and consider the many ways in which you touch me,
when I feel tears prick my eyes
and consider the many ways in which you challenge me,
I catch my breath, in wonder and in awe,
and ask for your forgiveness
for the times when I think I can control you.

God of many names and none
we come to you in awe and wonder,   Amen

Jill Thornton

CHAPTER ONE

HAS THE CHURCH A FUTURE?

Change is in the air! Everywhere I go in the United Reformed Church, people are talking about it, confirming our need for it and, even, starting to envisage it. Change is on the agenda of local churches, pastorate groups, District Councils and Synods. And it all gets focussed for us in the so-called Cornick Review. There is a guarded expectancy among us concerning that Review Group's findings, but I sense that people want action – forthright decisions which will put some much-needed life into us, some radical proposals to provide us with a renewed vision and a fresh purpose. To be sure, the realistic side of me causes me to wonder whether our plural church will be able to arrive at a common mind concerning what changes are needed – already we have seen adjacent Synods proposing to re-organize themselves in quite opposite ways. Nevertheless, I'm allowing the idealistic side of me to hold sway for the moment: the church seems to have the will to change, albeit prompted by membership rolls that are in free-fall and most certainly not fully aware of what the changes might entail. We can thank God: the United Reformed Church is preparing itself to be 'reformed'.

The situation we are facing as a church has been described by some as a crisis. All the evidence I have gathered moving around the churches of the North of England of late suggests that the word 'crisis' is perfectly appropriate, provided that we understand the word in its root meanings. The word 'crisis' comes from the Greek *krisis*, which, on the one hand, means 'judgement', but, on the other hand, also means to be in the 'right', as in 'justice' or 'righteousness'. 'Crisis', therefore, involves a clear recognition of what is wrong with us, but it also invites us to focus more positively on what is right about us. When used of the contemporary situation, the word need not only refer to negative judgements about the current state of our churches and denomination, but it also should point us in the opposite direction, attending to and grasping new opportunities excitedly and with fresh hope. If we understand our crisis in that kind of even-handed way we can view our contemporary predicament within the United Reformed Church as God-given: most certainly a word of judgement to us about what is wrong with us, but also an invitation to fresh discipleship made possible by God's forgiveness of us. The evidence around us may bring us close to despair, but faith is the generator of hope and new possibilities.

We only grow up when we realise that one day we will be no more. Death casts a shadow over our earthly existence, one that highlights those aspects of our lives that are most significant and lastingly important. To be sure, when young we live as if our years on earth are endless, but the moment comes when we are confronted with the fact that we are 'beings-born-unto-death' (Heidegger). Then, but not until then, we start to gain a realistic sense of values and establish real priorities. So it is with institutions, including churches. As long as they remain blind to their temporal reality, they easily lose a sense of purpose amid their helter-skelter existence, find that their priorities get skewed, and then complacency quickly sets in. But when they stare oblivion in the face institutions can become motivated to sow seeds for successful and creative times.

In our discussions, I sense that most of us agree the United Reformed Church has a future. No less an authority than our General Secretary believes that to be the case: 'God has not done with us yet', he has assured us. But a General Secretary would say that to his organisation, wouldn't he? What I want to suggest is that, for very good theological reasons, the United Reformed Church does not possess a future in any long-term sense, that for equally good sociological and historical reasons the United Reformed Church does not have a future in its present form and with its current outlook, and, finally, that only once these facts penetrate, will we then be in a position to think relevantly about what it means to be a faithful church.

I turn therefore to the theological, sociological and historical reasons which support my argument.

Theological Reflections: Only God is Eternal!

Lest we are tempted to start claiming too much for ourselves, Christians ought to maintain a healthy distinction between the temporal and the eternal, the universe created by God and God who created the universe. Anything which comes within the temporal arena bounded by creation is finite, i.e. it one day was not and it one day will be no more. What is essentially temporal can only be liberated from its temporality if God chooses to make it part of the divine life – and then it will have to undergo such a redemptive change that once in the divine life it will no longer possess all the old inadequacies it had in the temporal realm. To apply this point to the church, note the way Christians have made a distinction between 'the saints on earth' and 'the saints in heaven', the 'visible' and the 'invisible' church. In other words, the church only possesses such permanence as God grants it when finally reformed it becomes 'the communion of saints'. So the Seer of Patmos makes a point of noting in his great vision of 'the new heaven and the new earth' that there will be 'no temple in the city', a reminder that whatever value institutional religion possesses it has no final place in the grand scheme of things. We await the time when the temple will be "the Lord God the Almighty and the Lamb" (Revelation 21: 22). No church has an ultimate future; each is merely a provisional instrument helping us get by until it will be no longer needed.

I now live in a house with a garden from the bottom of which one can engineer a view of Durham Cathedral. All rather grand – and the birds sing in Durham, they used to cough in Manchester! But one does not have to reflect over much on the magnificence of Durham Cathedral's architecture to realize that some Christians have seen their churches less as 'provisional instruments' to engage with the Reign of God and more as permanent statements of the pre-eminence of their culture-mixed up as their culture invariably was with the secular as well as the sacred. And, lest I may appear to be claiming the high moral ground at this point, the Free Churches have not avoided doing similar things, as all the neo-Gothic additions to our churches during the Victorian era amply testify. The Old Testament reveals, though, that God's people are essentially a wandering, pilgrim people, always destined to live in the tension between remaining true to their 'tabernacle' heritage and seeking more permanent 'temple'–like structures. Today, this tension between 'tent' and 'temple' remains; indeed, nearly all our financial problems stem from an ongoing commitment to keep us in the temple traditions of our forebears, when most things belonging to that tradition are in fact crumbling before our very eyes.

We are now in a 'tabernacle' period of Christian history. Once again we are being called to travel light, no longer carrying yokes of bricks and mortar around our necks, but learning to live simply so that we can simply live. This is not to say that church buildings are unimportant, only to say that a great many of the buildings we struggle to keep going are no longer needed by us. It is to say, though, that now is the time to turn some of the resources that we possess in buildings into finance to support Christian mission among those who have turned their backs on what they see our many buildings standing for.

Unless I'm mistaken it was the intention of the United Reformed Church in 1972 to travel light, motivated by a belief that we were not so much called to become a new denomination on the British church scene but a catalyst for further union among the churches. At every Ordination and Induction service we say:

We affirm our intention
to go on praying and working,
with all our fellow Christians,
for the visible unity of the Church
in the way Christ chooses,
so that people and nations
may be led to love and serve God
and praise him more and more for ever.

The United Reformed Church was never meant to be permanent. Our ecumenical commitment underwrote a wider realization that the Saints on earth are always destined to die that they may be reborn: *semper reformanda et reformata*.

Our calling to travel light though should not be misunderstood. It must not involve a watered-down faith; it ought not to flirt with sloppy and careless patterns of worship; it cannot support laissez-faith attitudes to political views which keep oppression and injustice as the status quo. But it could mean our being liberated from being held captive by buildings and structures which we largely serve rather than they any longer serving us. And whatever we make of the ecumenical theology which fuelled the birth of the United Reformed Church, Paul's powerful question still needs asking amidst all the denominational competition so common on the Church scene: "Has Christ been divided?" (1 Corinthians 1: 13). And, even if that question does not set some of us on our ecumenical journey, surely we can all recognize that there are pressing economic, strategic and practical reasons why we should find ways of pooling resources and acting together. I suspect that the United Reformed Church cannot afford, *literally* cannot afford, to carry on as if we have a long-term future.

Sociological Reflections: Mission to Believers who do not belong

The advent of the PC has made all of us statistically inclined, prone to number-crunching if not quite becoming amateur social scientists. Hardly a day goes by without coming across a line of thinking totally dependent upon computer predictions. Did you know that if the United Reformed Church continues to decline at the present rate it will no longer exist by 2020? Equally, you ought to know that, using similar reasoning, predictions in 1880 regarding the rise of horse-drawn transport would have suggested that by 1920 London would have been buried under a foot of horse manure! Computer predictions like these assume steady-state conditions and do not take account of the checks and balances needed when parameters change through fresh initiatives. They also increase the possibility that we judge the worth-whileness of things by reference to 'quantity' at the expense of an appreciation of their 'quality'. If we adopt that line of approach with the church we soon run the risk of equating numerical strength with success (and, therefore, we render the most successful event in history a total waste of time and space: the life and death of Jesus of Nazareth!).

In the right hands social science can be very instructive for the Christian church, even if some of its theories require us to follow a principle learned on our Mother's knee – chew well before digesting. For example, the advent of Enlightenment values, which gave us all permission to question given authorities and think for ourselves, has not meant the end of religion as some cavalierly suggested. Actually, as sociologists like Grace Davie claim, there is a surprising amount of 'believing' around, even if people are not usually found exploring their spiritual awareness and searching for the Transcendent through the channels of mainstream churches. Levels of 'belonging' suggest a clear decline in the extent to which people take part in traditional religious practices and articulate their beliefs in ways that conform to traditional Christian thinking, but, quite surprisingly, new patters of religious devotion have been emerging through which people's 'believing' is being expressed.[1] Nevertheless, we should not make too much of this since the role of religion is now largely peripheral to our culture's institutions and the social standing of the churches is not what it used to be. The presence of 'belief' among so many people certainly ought not to blind us to the fact that the shape of their belief is not within hailing distance of Christian orthodoxy.[2] We are now part of a plural religious scene in which the old Christian hegemony has been fundamentally broken. The removal of Establishment, the last unfinished bit of the Reformation, seems inevitable irrespective of whether or not more local events tear the Church of England asunder.

We have moved from Christendom to a multi-religious culture in which the truth of what we believe cannot be assumed but now must be argued for, and the relevance and appropriateness of many of our social and political commitments are not just questioned but outwardly opposed. Our post-modern world is a mission field in which we cannot assume that people have a prior knowledge about the gospel or any awareness of our liturgical ways. When most of our contemporaries enter churches they encounter a culture alien to them. Their needs are largely unknown to us. We continue, though, to structure church life on the basis of

---

[1]   See Grace Davie, *Religion in Britain since 1946: Believing Without Belonging* (Oxford UK & Cambridge USA: Blackwell, 1994).

[2]   See Steve Bruce, *God is Dead: Secularization in the West* (Oxford: Blackwell Publishing, 2002).

---

what were people's needs in the Christendom era, with the result that we are usually way off addressing what contemporary 'believers' are looking for: perhaps inviting them for fellowship when they are actually looking for faith, focussing upon providing them with a social life when they actually want to deepen their spirituality, or asking them to help run ailing organisations when they are crying out for help in organising their lives? To put it very crudely: the church's 'product' increasingly does not match the needs of our clientele!

As I talk to people outside the church I discover people of mainly two types: 'half-believers' who find the elaborate doctrinal systems of the church either a contradiction of what they believe or an over-elaboration of it, and 'latent-believers' who find difficulty in connecting what they are all about with what they perceive to be the essence of institutional Christianity. Listen to a prominent spokesperson from each group. First, Dennis Potter the dramatist who, shortly before he died of cancer, was asked by Melvyn Bragg whether he had "any feeling that life might be eternal", given that Potter had once admitted that he'd "never quite thrown off the idea of believing in God":

> Yeah, God's a rumour if you like. I mean the kind of Christianity – or indeed any other religion – that is a religion because of fear of death or hope that there is something beyond death does not interest me. What kind of cruel old bugger is God, if it's terror that is the structure of religion. Religion has always been the wound, not the bandage. I don't see the point of not acknowledging the pain and the misery and the grief of the world. I see God in us or with us, if I see at all: some knowledge that we have, some feeling why we sing and dance and act, why we love, why we make art .[3]

Secondly, listen to Jonathon Parrott, the environmentalist:

> I think we can still discern today an enormous need for some kind of spiritual fulfilment and spiritual meaning, a need to look beyond the material confines within which most of our life is pitched. It's difficult to pin down: dogmatize that kind of feeling, try and classify it, try and pigeonhole it, by putting a bit of pretentious polysyllabic nomenclature to it, and it just blows away. Theologians don't like this, but this kind of spiritual yearning is not so much an intellectual abstraction as a powerfully felt gut-feeling, a metaphorical throb of the heart.[4]

---

[3]   *The Guardian,* 06.04.1994.
[4]   Quoted by Ruth Page in *God and the Web of Creation* (London: SCM Press, 1996), p 110.

To be sure, there are also those around who do not seem to give a damn about anything, but my experience is that people are more susceptible to the gospel than we usually assume, even if they often have not the slightest interest in the church as it is now constituted. Somehow we have to re-shape being church to fit the needs of this missionary hour, recognizing that, amidst all our orderliness and traditions, we desperately need, as the Apostle Paul recognized, to "become all things to all people, that [we] might by all means save some" (I Corinthians 9: 22). And am I alone in thinking that, like Paul in Athens, I must honour the unknown God worshipped by others as the prelude to a real dialogue with them? (Acts 17: 16-34). What now makes up the United Reformed Church seems ill-equipped to reach those of 'half-belief' or 'latent-belief', let alone the few who have no belief. In the present form, therefore, it, possesses no long-term future.

Historical Reflections: The Sins of the Parents visited upon the Children

The church history we have been taught was written up largely from the perspective of Western Christianity. For example, how affirming of our calling it once was to receive reports from overseas missionaries on furlough about the spread of the gospel in their particular neck of the woods. Now we know the price local cultures often had to pay in the process. It was only when I started reading books from the perspective of North American Indians that I realized that the sailing of the Mayflower led to an outrageous sequence of human oppression and brutality, as well as ecological destruction, when the Puritans of New England marched West, believing that, as members of the Elect, they had to 'Christianize' everything that lay in their way. I once believed that Christianity always leads to what is good and wholesome; but now I often have difficulty equating the good news of Jesus Christ with the performance of institutional Christianity. We have a very poor track record, but so have other religions. Polly Toynbee has launched a tirade against all religion:

> [Religion] is there in the born-again Christian fundamentalism demanded of every US politician, turning them all into "Crusaders". It drives on the murderous Islamic jihad's. It makes mad the biblical land-grabbing Israeli settlers. It threatens nuclear nemesis between Hindus and Muslims along the India-Pakistan border. It hurls pipe-bombs on the Ulster streets. The Falun Gong are killed for it, extremist Sikhs die for it. The Pope kills millions through his reckless spreading of Aids. When absolute God-given righteousness beckons blood flows and women are in chains.[5]

---

[5]   Quoted by David R. Peel in *Ministry for Mission* (Manchester: Northern College, 2003), pp 13-14.

Do not assume any longer that people think well of us. We now have to re-earn the respect some of our past activities have removed.

Also, our place in society is no longer assured in the way it once was. To be sure, religion under New Labour is fêted, mainly because Britain's religious institutions possess a significant record of being able to deliver very basic local social services more efficiently, humanely, and, here's the real reason, with voluntary labour more cost-effectively than the State. But, aside from this, as Alistair Campbell has said, the government doesn't do religion! We should rejoice that locally the church often remains the sole focus for neighbourliness, and, that nationally, we still attempt to be some kind of social conscience; but we now only seem to score well when we are being explicitly non-religious. And, if that is the case, we have unearthed a further reason why the United Reformed Church has little future as presently constituted.

The Way Ahead

In the light of the evidence, we are driven to ask: What is the United Reformed Church here to do – given that what we are now doing seems to have precious little future? Allow me to sketch an answer in three parts.

First, our starting point is to become what the church is meant to be: a sign, expression and foretaste of God's kingdom. We are called to that shape of life which comes about when a community of people attempts to work in harmony with God's will for the world and finds what it says and does increasingly radiating the life of the Triune God : the power of love behind, within and beyond all things. We have to recognize that we are very much a means to an end. Our calling is to engage in God's mission *(missio Dei)*. Anything we do in the church's life which does not serve that mission – or, more to the point, puts obstacles in our way as we seek to get involved in it – is surplus to the church's requirements. When we assemble for worship, it is to be prepared for mission; when we engage with the church's teaching it is to learn what we are to say and to do when we are asked to give an account of the hope that is within us (I Peter 3: 15); when we support one another in prayer it is to help us all possess the strength to live out our Christian vocations in our homes, at the work place and in our leisure activities. If we can no longer fulfil our role in God's mission, then we have already forfeited our right to be a church, simply because we have reached the stage when we can no longer fulfil the purpose for which we have been set apart. Am I all that far off in thinking that some of congregations are now precisely in this position: their work now finished, what they were called to do now at an end, their life over?

A return to our missionary roots undoubtedly will involve a will to travel light and, hence, become liberated from many of the structures and practices which now are oppressing us. But our deep-seated problem is greater than a lack of appropriate structures. To pretend that the much-needed reformation of the United Reformed Church will be achieved by structural change is akin to re-arranging the deck-chairs on the Titanic. What we most desperately need is a renewal of our faith in the gospel, so that we know what we believe and stand for and, yes, what we would be prepared to die for. So the second thread of my answer concerning the future of the United Reformed Church focuses upon the faith which must undergird our mission and the need for the church to be so constituted that we are enabled, empowered and encouraged to develop that faith. I find it striking how much time lively churches – whether here or overseas – pay to bible study, theological reflection, preaching and teaching. They wrap their church life around an on-going discovery of the significance of the life, teaching, death and resurrection of Jesus for themselves and their society. Isn't it time for the congregations of the United Reformed Church to attend to the basics which underpin our missionary faith: matters of faith and belief? How else can we learn to connect with the 'half-believers' and the 'latent-believers' who do not yet belong? What other way is there to get in a position to know what might be involved in living a Christian life in contemporary society? We must liberate churches from that deathly church culture PT Forsyth once dismissed as 'short sermons and long socials'.[6]

It follows that, thirdly, what this hour requires in the United Reformed Church are designated ministries that can lead us to rediscover a missionary focus rooted in a rigorous faith. The onus that this places on ministers of Word and Sacraments (whether stipendiary or non-stipendiary, full-time or part-time) is great. They will need to possess theological acumen, educational ability and understanding of the world and culture so that they can help church members recall with gratitude the faith tradition in which they stand and thus re-tell their faith story in ways that can be 'heard' by their contemporaries. This 'high' Reformed view of ministry can only be sustained if those called to partner ministries in the church also play their full part. Acting together, the church's different ministries do not exist to do the church's work, but rather to put the church to work. We ought also to expect our Elders to play a more central and significant role, since at present in many congregations the ministry of the Elder regrettably seems to involve little more than membership of a committee! Meanwhile, ways of deploying stipendiary ministers need urgent attention, with a recognition that local church leadership will have to be focused elsewhere – in people ministers equip, enable and empower.[7]

---

6   See P T Forsyth's, *Positive Preaching and the Modern Mind* (London: Independent Press Ltd., 1964) for the view that "a Christianity of short sermons is a Christianity of short fibre" (p 75).

7   For further development of this theme see my *Ministry for Mission*.

The thesis of this address has been that the United Reformed Church possesses a limited future, not least due to our ecumenical commitments. In the time God has left for us we need to re-vision and re-structure so that our life and work serves God's missionary purposes. Essential to this task will be discovering afresh what we are called to be in society, and to help make this possible we need well-prepared and well-supported ministries which will once again make the church work.

CHAPTER TWO

A CHURCH FOR A NON-CHURCH CULTURE

Acts 11: 1-18

Page in Arizona is a new town formed following the damming of the Colorado River and the creation of Lake Powell, an act of environmental vandalism. It has produced a new water sports and recreational area of considerable beauty. Page is a growing town set amidst an Indian reservation. It has been created solely to service the leisure industry. Everything is new. We stayed in a motel on the outskirts of the town. The road into the centre of the town had on the left-hand side all the town's schools and medical centres and on the right hand side all its churches. There were eleven of them, I seem to remember – eleven churches of different flavour: Mormon to Roman Catholic, Presbyterian to Episcopalian. Every religious persuasion is catered for – and all on the same street. This represents religious provision for a consumerist culture. But what, I asked myself, becomes of the unity of the church in this town? All the row of eleven churches in Page, Arizona has in common would seem to be the common parking lot at the rear. The different churches which are dotted on the landscapes of our villages, towns and cities may not stand in a line as in Page, but they are usually equally as independent and they provide choice for practising Christians – even if sometimes they are not yet in the habit of sharing their parking lot!

We can almost take for granted that there is nothing wrong in Christian diversity – provided it doesn't spill over into a form of competitiveness which leads to disharmony and disunity. That was not the case during the early years of Christianity, particularly when things were viewed from the perspective of the Mother Church in Jerusalem. After all, Jerusalem was the seat of authentic Christianity – or so it seemed to the members of that church.

'Authentic Christianity' – *the* one true tradition, *the* one proper worshipping practice, *the* one authoritative Christian way of life, how exclusivist claims have littered Christian history, whether it be Constantinian Roman, Eastern Byzantium, Reformed Protestant, Elizabethan English, or whatever version. How can it be possible for anyone to be a true Christian if they do not believe what we believe, worship as we do or share our lifestyle? A friend of the family defiantly proclaimed that she was born a Congregationalist and would die a Congregationalist. The problem for me, a teenager at the time, was that her determination to be authentically Christian seemed to bypass most of what Christianity involved. She hadn't even entered the world of the shared parking-lot, though the disease isn't confined to Congregationalists.

Peter must have suffered from it for a time. He grew up in the early years of the Jerusalem church to believe that authentic Christianity – although he wouldn't have used the term – was confined to the congregation of Jews who had accepted Jesus as their Lord. And yet, away from Jerusalem, in Gentile towns and cities a different kind of Christianity was emerging due to the missionary activity of Paul. This version of Christianity, unlike the Jerusalem version, did not insist that potential members had to become circumcised or adhere to Jewish food laws, while it permitted marriage even though Christ's coming was imminently expected, and it also possessed a more liberal attitude to the role of women within the church. It was a version which shocked Peter and the Jerusalem church. They knew what authentic Christianity looked like, and it wasn't what was in evidence in places like Philippi, Antioch and Corinth – why, in Corinth, Christians were even eating food which before going on the butcher's slab had been offered to idols!

It took a vision to move Peter on from his entrenched, exclusivist understanding to accept that Gentile cars could be parked on the Jerusalem church car park. At Joppa, he learned that "God has given even to the Gentiles the repentance that leads to life" (Acts 11: 18). But the suspicion and hostility between the two versions of Christianity which emanate from the respective missionary activities of Peter and Paul rumbled on through the early years of the church's life, the Council at Jerusalem mentioned later in Acts not withstanding (15: 1-29). Viewed from one side, what was happening in the Gentile world was a departure from true Christianity; viewed from the other side, what was happening was the expression of the gospel in a non-Jewish culture – what scholars these days rather grandly refer to as 'inculturalization', giving the Good News a set of clothes appropriate to a different culture. If what some Christians regarded as unorthodox and inauthentic had not taken place, it is possible that Christianity would never have spread outside Jerusalem.

But we enjoy *our* 'Jerusalem', the theology, worship and practice which is *our* way of doing things, the clothes in which the gospel was dressed when it came to us. Just as Gentiles were different to Jews, so, today, those outside the church are mainly alien from the Christian culture, our words and ways, our traditions and habits. About half the people in our society have not had serious contact with church culture for up to three generations in their families, so our church world is as foreign to them as Jewish culture was to first century Gentiles. What is quite clear is that if the gospel is going to reach those outside the church, we will have courageously to liberate it from the culture in which it is set, and allow it to take root and find new life in the non-church culture of these people. This will not be easy, just as it was not easy for Peter who also had to accept new ways of being church as valid.

One of the reasons why Christianity has been so successful around the world is that it has been capable of re-inventing itself for radically different contexts. We can with hindsight respect the need of missionaries who had to find new ways of being church in far away cultures. We find it less easy to contemplate that we now have to find similar new ways for a post-modern culture which has largely by-passed the church. We are as tied to our traditions as Peter was to his. The vision at Joppa opened his eyes to a wider view of the church. He realized that Christ can meet people on *their* terms; they did not first have to become Jews. We also must hold on to the belief that, today, Christ will encounter people at the heart of their cultural identities; they do not first have to share our church culture. Like Peter, we must sow the seeds for a church beyond *our* church. Today is a new era, one that will demand its own church in the way Gentiles once demanded theirs. We must learn to share the parking lot with an unchurched culture.

PART TWO
AN ENCOUNTERING CHURCH

WORSHIP FOCUS: CHILDREN

**Jesus said: 'Unless you have faith like a little child,
                        you will not enter the kingdom of heaven.'**

During the 9th Assembly of the World Council of Churches held in Brazil, Finnish Lutherans posed the question "What did Jesus see in children?" Participants from all over the world were asked to respond from their own experience of children.

Here are some of their answers:

- *Hong Kong* – Spirituality should be simple and playful, with all honesty. Children have that.

- *Brazil* – Children are spontaneously confident.

- *Netherlands* – Children are mature spiritually because they are open and respectful and dare to be vulnerable.

- *Namibia* – The child is characterized by stubborn trust and the ability to change and forgive.

- *Switzerland* – Children are always open to be surprised.

PRAYER

Think of a child's hands
playing with bubbles in a kitchen sink . . .

Childlike God, encourage me to be playful;
not constrained by how things 'ought' to be,
but free to explore how things can be.

Think of a child putting their hand up
because they are bursting with the answer to a question . . .

Childlike God, inspire me with confidence;
so that I may share the good news
with all whom I meet.

Think of a child's hands
reaching up to be held . . .

Childlike God, strengthen me to be vulnerable;
open to drawing on my own weaknesses
to minister to another.

Think of a child holding hands
with a grown-up to cross the road . . .

Childlike God, help me to trust you;
even when I can't see the big picture
and my path is difficult.

Think of a child's hands
opening a gift . . .

continue overleaf ...

Prayer continued ...

Childlike God, challenge me to be open to surprises;
never to be so comfortable in my faith
that I cannot be filled with anticipation and wonder.

Playful
Confident
Vulnerable.
Trusting
Surprising God
we offer this prayer to you
in the name of the baby,
born in a manger,   Amen.

Jill Thornton

CHAPTER THREE

A FRAMEWORK FOR AN ENCOUNTERING CHURCH

The United Reformed Church has committed itself to *Catch the Vision:* a radical review of our life and activity. The *Catch the Vision* process is a key moment in our life. It is a time to face words of judgement as well as feed upon words of grace; an opportunity to become open to what God has for us to do; a chance to re-shape ourselves so that we are a sign, expression and anticipation of God's power, presence and promise; an invitation to reconstitute ourselves so that we can faithfully fulfil our calling to re-present to others the claim which is placed upon the lives of everyone and the whole cosmos by God. Above all else, *Catch the Vision* is *the* occasion within the short life of the United Reformed Church when we have been given the opportunity prayerfully and humbly to await the work God has for us, as we plumb the rich depths of scripture and tradition in order to be led by the Spirit into fresh ways of being church. What does it mean to be an encountering church whose local congregations make a difference to the lives of people, societies and even the world? *That* mission, God's invitation to become a people who encounter others with a distinctive message and way of life, will only become clear to us as we renew our encounter with God.

A. The Real Driving Force for Contemporary Mission

> We are not to be driven by guilt concerning our decline nor by a desire to give people what they want; rather, mission is our thankful response to what God graciously supplies for our need.

As we struggle to be a faithful church, we are often pushed forward today by two driving forces: on the one hand our most recent performances of being church and on the other the social and cultural upheavals we are facing. Both need treating with caution.

Concerning the first driving force, we know that the zenith of Nonconformity came in the middle of the nineteenth century and that thereafter our church tradition has been in numerical decline, with a marked increase in the rate of that decline from the 1960s onwards. While we must beware of equating ecclesial health with numerical strength, the statistics clearly do not lie completely.

Nevertheless, our experience of decline is heightened by a Victorian legacy, namely, the material results of an obsession for church building without giving due attention to population movement. This has left us with far too many church buildings where we don't need them and arguably a lack of them in some places where we now require them. Often, the institutional competitiveness generated by wealthy Independent Christians simply added to the over-provision of church plant in the Free Church constituency. I am told that in Heckmondwike during a supposed hey-day of Nonconformity that, with a little squeezing, the three Independent chapels could accommodate the entire seven thousand population between them as though there were no other denomination there at all!

It may also be the case that as membership rolls plummet numbers of adherents in our congregations are rising, but, when we are finished with analysing the statistics, the bottom line is simply this, if I may risk possible accusations of ageism: my generation and that of my children are largely missing from most of our congregations. Going to church these days is one of the few places where I still feel young! Unless we accept the ridiculous notion that church-going is largely a retirement activity, we must find ways of attracting a much wider age-range. Our motivation for doing that, however, ought not to be a deep worry about how we can keep the institution called 'church' alive; rather, it should be a Spirit-driven conviction rising phoenix-like out of the dying embers of past ways of being Church and generating a felt need to draw others into the abundant generosity of God's love.

Secondly, and concerning the other driving force, the culture within which our mission now has to be set has been in a tremendous state of upheaval during my lifetime. Treasured values, traditions and institutions no longer hold sway as perhaps once was the case. However, in a culture in which 'heritage' is a niche market, we need to note the way in which our perceptions about change often veer towards nostalgia. It is easy to view the past in a more positive light that it actually deserves and thereby to react to the present rather more negatively than is helpful.

What has happened to Christian believing and the institutional church is a good example of the seismic changes we are facing. Where once Christian teaching could be taken as read, we can no longer take it for granted that what we believe will be accepted in a vibrant multi-faith society. We now find ourselves having to enter into dialogue with others and argue our case sensitively. Nor does the church possess the standing in society it once did. In fact, a major challenge today concerns how we address those who dismiss us as irrelevant, or who have given up on us because of what they perceive are our sexist, racist or homophobic tendencies. While many people are at best critical or at worst apathetic to the church, they still often react positively to the words and witness of Jesus, and it remains significant that in a so-called secular age they still search for personal fulfilment in a 'spiritual' realm that they clearly believe lies beyond all the seemingly unfulfilled hopes of their 'material' world.

It could be that people who at present are hostile or indifferent to us because of the way we "do" church would be interested and committed to new forms of being church, ones that seek to be faithful to Jesus at one and the same time as attempting to be relevant in our age. There undoubtedly is a world of spiritual searching beyond the church to which the church needs to respond with some urgency. Nevertheless, we must beware of 'dumbing' the gospel down to what our individualistic culture will find acceptable. Authentic, cross-bearing discipleship challenges a great deal in current society's ethos. Bonhoeffer warned us against operating with 'cheap grace'. Equally, we need to avoid living off 'stale grace', perceptions and practices which have lost touch with the counter-cultural essence of the Christian witness of faith. A key to a faithful future will be our ability to re-learn the art and normality of swimming against the tide.

B.   Local Church Programmes and Conciliar Frameworks for Mission

The national church cannot prescribe for a local congregation, but it fails its duty if it does not provide a framework within which faithful ways of being church can be created appropriate to local contexts.

We are being called and challenged to find patterns of obedience through which people will encounter Church in what we are saying and doing. But that will only be possible if we break through the insularity which so often holds us captive in order to become an encountering church, one which has relearned that mission, understood in its most inclusive sense, is the very *raison d'être* of the church. I never agreed with Bishop Lesslie Newbigin's analysis of contemporary society, finding it unduly negative and his prescriptions for our ills unnecessarily exclusivist and damagingly dogmatic. But I have never forgotten a passage from his *Honest Religion for Secular Man* which I read when a science undergraduate:

The church . . . has listened to the words 'Come unto me', but not listened to the words 'Go-and I am with you'. It has interpreted election as if it meant being chosen for special privilege in relation to God, instead of being chosen for special responsibility before God for other men. It has interpreted conversion as if it was simply a turning towards God for purposes of one's own private inner religious life, instead of seeing conversion as it is in the Bible, a turning towards God for the doing of His will in the secular world. It has understood itself more as an institution than as an exhibition. Its typical shape in the eyes of its own members as well as those outside has been not a band of pilgrims who have heard the word 'Go', but a large and solid building which, at its best, can only say 'Come', and at its worst says, all too clearly, 'Stay away' [8]

And, yes, let's face it; we have far too many buildings at the moment which tell people to 'stay away'!

What would the 'encountering church' I'm advocating actually look like? It will be a community which makes a difference to people and the world around it and beyond; its focus will be the empowering and equipping of young and old to live Christ-like lives in their ordinary encounters at home, work and play; it will invite people 'in' in order to send them 'out' more confident and hopeful; it will be a thorn in the flesh of all unjust structures and practices. But it may be asked, what of its programme? For several reasons, I do not think that it is Assembly business to determine such a programme. That task belongs to each covenanting collection of God's saints in the context which is uniquely theirs. Different times will require different emphases, as will different age and interest groups – one size will not fit all! Nor can we prescribe from a distance if we take local church contexts seriously. Mission after the example of Christ needs to be more 'bottom up' than 'top down', otherwise it so easily becomes manipulative and insensitive. Everything rests therefore with the ability of local outcroppings of gathered saints to be signs and sacraments of God's acceptance and generosity in their gloriously ordinary lives and communities. Lying underneath this observation, of course, is our Reformed conviction that all the marks of the true church can indeed be found within a faithful local congregation.

While a programme for the encountering church must be hammered out at a local congregational level, the fact that each congregation is in fellowship with other similar congregations through the Councils of the church suggests a role for the wider church in facilitating their work. Collectively we might devise a broad framework within which local programmes for encountering church can be developed, as well as suggest key areas for churches to work on as they strive for missionary effectiveness. In what follows I will offer some suggestions concerning a framework for local church mission as well as delineate those key areas in church life which most need our renewed attention. While I will not have time to develop

---

[8]   Lesslie Newbigin, *Honest Religion for Secular Man* (London: SCM Press, 1966), pp 101-102.

---

my thinking on these key areas in this address, I hope to work on them with the members of this year's Holiday Forum and during my visits around the United Reformed Church constituency.

C.   A Framework for the Life and Witness of a Local Church

Six interlocking themes to aid the missionary planning of the local church.

I'm presenting this framework for wider discussion within the *Catch the Vision* process in the conviction that before we get immersed in all the structural and practical proposals starting to flow from our review it will be prudent if we attend to primary issues concerning what the church is called to become if we are to be faithful participants in God's mission.   My first theme fundamentally underpins all the others; there is no significance in the order of priority of the rest.

1.   An Appropriate View of God

The God on display in many churches is not the lively God of the Christian tradition.

We need to recapture the art of finding the Transcendent within our daily activities, locating God's ways within the midst of our worldly ways, reading 'the signs of the times' to re-engage with the One who always is doing new things.[9]   What we say and do as Christians should re-present to others not only God's invitation to enjoy the divine generosity of being the chosen, accepted and forgiven sons and daughters of God and but also God's challenge to take up the responsibilities towards others that are placed upon us.   The vision of the kingdom God has set before us in the Christ event thus presents us with the model God expects us to adopt in all our personal and corporate affairs.

Blaise Pascal once remarked that the God of Abraham, Isaac and Jacob is not the God of the philosophers and scholars.   Some 'philosophers and scholars', of course, have come closer to the biblical picture of God than those Pascal had in mind, while the church has often been at its most obscurantist when reacting to scientific and technological developments.   Be that as it may, adapting Pascal's claim a little, there is a strong case for suggesting that God, the One who is with all beings and things as Creator, became incarnate in the Redeemer and gives life to all through the Spirit, is a far cry from the 'God' being exhibited in the life and witness of many contemporary

---

9   Isaiah 43: 16-21; Matthew 16: 1-4. (All scripture references are taken from the *New Revised Standard Version* 1989, copyright of the Division of Christian Education of the National Council of Churches of Christ in the United States of America.)

Christian churches. How easily we have transformed the grandeur of God into the narrow-mindedness of a tribal Deity. We have reduced a cosmic Deity to a Christian god – as if the mission of God in Jesus concerned only Christians rather than the whole world. How common it has also been for us to exchange the incarnate Deity who became 'down-to-earth' in Jesus for an altogether more distant God, who, aloof from our everyday material world, conveniently never engages with either our personal or political affairs. Our Nonconformist forebears would be turning in their graves! Frightened by the vitality and diversity of God, we even end up pretending that God creates everything the same in all the ways we just happen to find comfortable. We trim 'God' down to fit our narrow mentality when what we ought to be doing is respond to the excitement of God, the One who not only says 'Yes' but sometimes 'No' to our ideas and ways, the One who challenges us to do new things in obedience, and the One who is forever surprising us with fresh possibilities.

The second theme of my framework follows from this need to display in our church life an altogether more lively understanding of God, one which is based upon a renewed experience of God in the midst of life:

2.   A Positive Attitude to Change

> 'The times, they are a changing' - they always have. Rejoice, for in the changes we find God!

God has created an evolving cosmos within which God's purposes are fleshed out. The Deity is endlessly finding new ways in which to relate to the world. God's love is unchanging, but the way in which that love is expressed at different times and places is relative to what is appropriate to those times and places. As Heraclitus is recorded as saying: 'Nothing is permanent but change', and, in certain ways, this insight applies even to God. Nevertheless, there exists within the Western psyche a long-standing prejudice against change. This goes right back to the Ancient Greeks who viewed perfection in terms of what is static and supposedly complete. This prejudice seeped into Christian piety, as the following lines from a well-known hymn testify:

> Swift to its close ebbs out life's little day;
> earth's joys grow dim, its glories pass away;
> change and decay in all around I see;
> O Thou who changest not, abide with me.[10]

---

[10]   From Henry F. Lyte's hymn 'Abide with me', found in *Rejoice and Sing* (Oxford: Oxford University Press, 1991), number 336.

Note how Lyte links 'change' with 'decay', thereby viewing 'change' totally negatively. Also observe how his understanding of God is not centred upon God's infinite ability to respond appropriately to evolving situations, and hence God's capacity in certain respects to change, but simply upon God's changelessness in the eternal aspect of the divine life.

Unlike the Greeks, however, we know that everything which exists is in a state of flux and hence changing – whether we think of the smallest building blocks of matter, persons, cultures or the whole cosmos. In terms of what we know, the static is a mere abstraction from reality, not perfection as the Greeks believed. Nor need change imply decay; it can also involve improvement, new levels of complexity and greater value. Process does not guarantee progress, but it sometimes does lead to it. To believe that yesterday was better than today is as simplistic as believing that the future will necessarily be better than the present. But the future can only be made better if we accept change as normative rather than resist it in principle.

Part of the genius of God lies in the way God works. The Creator has produced an evolving universe that is largely self-determining, yet through patient initiatives the divine Will is exercised as the created order responds to divine prompting. The very least God's subjects ought to do is to engage positively with change, conceiving fresh futures grounded in the belief that the world can be made a better place. There is much to be learned from the notion that to live is to change, and to live well is to have changed often. It is striking how the world's best minds undergo not only developments in their ideas but sometimes have dramatic sea-changes of view. This is particularly true of Christian theologians.

The future is bright – not because it's Orange but because it belongs to God. And God, because God is God, can cope with whatever the future brings! Only a positive attitude to change can provide us with a hope for the future to underpin our commitment to the present. When "change" is believed necessarily to involve "decay" we cannot have any realistic hope this side of eternity; but when "change" is viewed more positively in terms of the myriad of possibilities for new life that it opens up we can possess hope in a future before as well as in Eternity. Our grounds for saying this lies in a healthy view of history, one which feeds upon the fact that, since God did not give up on folk in the past, we can be confident that God will be with us 'through all the changing scenes of life'. This takes us to our third theme in my framework:

3.   A Critical Approach to Tradition

Beware of 'traditionalism'; embrace 'tradition'

The Christian tradition contains a fair amount of dross surrounding the vitally precious nuggets that give us continuity with the great stream of witness which began with the earliest confessors of Christ as Saviour and Lord. Our task is to remove the dross so that the nuggets can once again shine in their full glory. My way of describing this perennial task is to speak of discerning the difference between "the living voice of tradition" and "the dead hand of traditionalism". We witness to our faith with the saints; therefore we do not have to make everything up as we go along. But it is never easy to separate the "tradition" of the saints from the "traditionalist" practices to which it has sometimes become wedded.

I'm certain that *Catch the Vision* is essentially about looking backwards in search of "living tradition"; but I'm equally clear that it involves setting to one side a whole host of things that are now surplus to our needs. Many of the so-called traditions of our congregations are recent accretions to their church life when viewed from the perspective of two thousand years of church history. They also can seem somewhat parochial when placed in a wider ecumenical context. The way some of our members defend their traditionalism to the death, though, is one of the more worrying aspects of our life. But of equal concern is the reluctance within our churches to plumb the depths of our "living tradition". There is a lack of urgency about engaging with the Bible and with the major themes of Christian theology. Fred Pratt Green has his finger on the pulse of a healthy attitude to tradition when he reminds us that:

> We need not now take refuge in tradition
> like those prepared to make a final stand,
> but use it as a springboard of decision,
> to follow him whose kingdom is at hand.[11]

Tradition will only become "a springboard of decision" when we receive it anew through renewed acquaintance with it. To further that end we need *theological* leadership from our ministers and an ongoing commitment from the church to invest in theological education across the churches. Fundamental to our current task is re-appropriating faith for our age.

---

[11]   From Fred Pratt Green's hymn 'Sing, one and all, a song of celebration', found in *Rejoice and Sing*, number 581.

4. A Relational View of Society

'The Word 'I' remains the shibboleth of humanity'.[12]

Ever since Margaret Thatcher announced that there is no such thing as society, and thereby gave the Prime Ministerial blessing to the culture of individualism, Christian commentators have come forward with persuasive critiques of our supposedly 'me myself and I' world. The more perceptive of them have noted the positive features of the society in which we now live. They highlight the way in which increasing human autonomy has made it possible for whole sections of humankind to experience once undreamed of freedoms, for example, women becoming liberated from the shackles of male domination and members of the two thirds world being set free from colonial bondage. Being truly an individual is a phenomenon many only recently have come near to acquiring, even though countless others have yet to experience it. However, as the better critiques argue, true individuality can only be fully attained in relationship with other individuals whose uniqueness in the sight of God is valued and affirmed. So, in Christian teaching, the path to becoming fully human is marked out by the twin demands of entering into loving relationships with not only God but also all those who place a claim upon our lives as neighbours.[13] This is a far cry from those forms of the contemporary quest for human autonomy which only give rise to an interest in the self and often precious little attention to the existence, let alone the needs, of others.

I say "often" since I do not want to get into the bad Christian habit of so emphasising what is wrong with the world that we fail to acknowledge its more wholesome aspects. If the overwhelming public response to the Boxing Day tsunami is anything to go by we might do well for once orientating our presentation of the gospel towards what is best in people rather than what is worst. Before we rabbit on about the evils of our fragmented world we ought to note that the public generosity following the tsunami was in fact, as *The Observer* stated, 'a mark of the connectedness of the world in which we live, whose far reaches are more familiar to us than to any other generation' .[14]

Increasingly, people are realising that, in a post 9/11 world, the most fundamental question facing humankind is that of global solidarity and togetherness. Not only is it clearly absurd to claim there is no such thing as society, it is profoundly dangerous to view the world in such a way that fear or even hatred

---

12   Martin Buber, *I and Thou* 3rd edn. (Edinburgh: T & T Clark, 1970) pp 115. 119.
13   See Luke 10: 25-37.
14   *The Observer*, 2 January 2005.

becomes the barrier to achieving the degree of "connectedness" which alone can guarantee world peace. Central to Christianity is the challenge to remove ourselves from the centre of our worlds and instead put God and others central. But the ideology of individualism also runs counter to the philosophy of the most significant Jewish thinker of the twentieth century. Martin Buber recognised that living in relationships with others is part of the very essence of our being fully human: 'All actual life is encounter', he proclaimed, thereby underscoring the view that the fully autonomous self is deficient.[15]

Part of Buber's complex thought is echoed in some memorable words from a former Bishop of Durham: 'I cannot be fully me until you are fully you, and that means that you must be you in such a way that it enables me to be me; and similarly I must be me in such a way that it enables you to be you'.[16] I find it increasingly challenging to realise that not only my thinking but my whole person is deficient and lacking unless I'm part of a fully reciprocal relationship with others who are different to me. It is through "the other" that I find myself. In relation with others I discover and develop; on my own I can only stagnate. I need the other's perspective: the perspective of women, children, blacks, gays and so on, since from my place in the world my understanding is partial. So if I wish to further my grasp of reality I need to learn from those who 'live' in different places and therefore perceive different things. This requires what Gordon Kaufman calls 'free-flowing, open, and unfettered conversation'.[17] We need to cultivate ways of sharing and living faith with others that open up the possibilities of learning faith from them – both inside and outside the Christian community.

5.   A Realistic Understanding of the Church

> But we have this treasure in clay jars, so that it may be made clear that this extraordinary power belongs to God and does not come from us.[18]

I have a love-hate relationship with the church. It has been my life in so many ways and helped shape who I am, but equally it has provided me with many bad nightmares – so much so that what often has kept me going has been the witness of

---

15   Buber, *I and Thou*, p 62.
16   David E. Jenkins, *God, Jesus and Life in the Spirit* (London: SCM Press, 1988), p 71.
17   Gordon D. Kaufman, *In Face of Mystery: A Constructive Theology* (Cambridge, Mass. and London: Harvard University Press, 1993), p 66. See also L. Swidler, J.B. Cobb Jr., P. F. Knitter and M. K. Hellwig, *Death or Dialogue? From the Age of Monologue to the Age of Dialogue* (London: SCM Press and Philadelphia: Trinity Press International, 1990), pp 56-77.
18   2 Corinthians 4: 7.

---

the Seer of Patmos in the Book of Revelation that in the Eternal City there will be no Temple, because at the End there will be no need for religion.[19] When church debate has been at its most quarrelsome, and our faithlessness has been most apparent, I have found it important to remember that the church is but the means to the End and not the End itself. We signify . . . we express . . . we anticipate, but this side of Eternity we never *are* the Kingdom. Let us never forget that the earthly church is a temporal means to an eternal End. Being temporal means being subject to all the forces of change as well as the final reality of death. Churches rise up and they pass away, as is the case with all temporal entities. We need to bear this in mind as we humbly set about the task of responding to the challenge of re-constituting ourselves afresh in ways appropriate to the gospel and relevant to our age.

The church is an all too human institution which is always in need of critical examination and reconstruction as it attempts to remain faithful to the Mystery it seeks to exhibit. In certain periods, it has expressed itself through solid, confident statements: magnificent buildings and articulate statements of faith. At other points in history, though, it has taken on an altogether more humble disposition, being more a pilgrim people than an institutional presence. We are now at the end of an ecclesiastical era, a period in which the institutional presence of the church at the heart of local communities was assured, with young and old being attracted into church life through any number of activities. That way of being church, with which we have become familiar, and due to which most of us are here at this Assembly, is no longer relevant to many of today's spiritual searchers. Just as our forebears found ways of being church which enabled the folk of their time to respond to the gospel, so we are called to a comparable task.

This will inevitably mean recognising that today 'people want to "live" experientially rather than "die" institutionally'.[20] They want "religion" or "spirituality", but they have little time for all the institutional trappings within which we currently present it. Sometimes, we fail to meet their needs because often we lack "imagination";[21] at other times, we simply refuse to adopt strategies of presenting the gospel which do not fit our styles or temperaments. 'Over my dead body', we hear it said. Well, given the age of most of our congregations we will not have to wait long!

---

[19]   See Revelation 21: 22.
[20]   Julius Lipner, "Religion and Religious Thinking in the New Millennium" in P. L. Wickeri, J. K. Wickeri and D.M.A. Niles eds., *Plurality, Power and Mission: Intercontextual Theological Explorations on the Role of Religion in the New Millennium* (London: The Council for World Mission, 2000), pp 88-89.
[21]   Lipner, "Religion and Religious Thinking in the New Millennium", p 89.

It will take a greater awareness of the temporal nature of the church for us to become open to whatever radical changes are now being called from our faithfulness. Many of our churches reflect the success and confidence of Nonconformity during the Victorian and Edwardian eras. We come from a "temple" culture when what we now perhaps need is a "tent" tradition which will bring us mobility and flexibility in a rapidly changing world: taking the church to where people now are rather than expecting them to come to us, expressing the gospel in response to people's current hopes and fears, and creating worship which addresses today's concerns and issues.

6. A Commitment to Life.

'I came that they may have life, and have it abundantly'.[22]

When at its best the church has interpreted its mission both "materially" and "spiritually", recognising that "abundant life" refers to this present life as well as to an existence beyond the present life. Christianity thereby has affirmed the importance of current social and political realities alongside the promise of the life hereafter in its understanding of what constitutes being fully human. Many has been the time when we have torn apart what really belongs together, with one wing of the church claiming that the gospel centres upon people getting right with God while the other insists that the gospel is all about Kingdom building in the here and now. We have sometimes given the impression that the United Reformed Church is better at the Kingdom building part of the gospel agenda. Fortunately, and increasingly, all but extreme "evangelicals" and "liberals" are seeing truths in their one-time opponents' positions.

In a very significant way, we need to be both "evangelical" and "liberal" if we are to present the gospel fully. John de Gruchy argues correctly that 'we have to find a way whereby appreciation for the mystery . . . of faith is kept in creative tension with our concern for social reality and concreteness'.[23] Indeed, if the United Reformed church were fully self-critical we would recognise a weakness on both sides: a lack of depth, the spirituality which comes from patiently waiting for God's voice as we attend to scripture, tradition and the words of one another, as well as a far from total commitment to "the impossible possibility" (Reinhold Niebuhr) of creating the Kingdom of God. Meanwhile, one clear feature of our

---

[22]   John 10: 10.
[23]   John W. de Gruchy, "Religion in the Millennium: A Christian Perspective" in P. L. Wickeri, J. K. Wickeri and D.M.A. Niles eds., *Plurality, Power and Mission: Intercontextual Theological Explorations on the Role of Religion in the New Millennium*. p 107.

age concerns the way in which past opposites and hierarchies such as 'reason and revelation', 'faith and science', 'clerics and laity', etc, as well as once unbridgeable divides of religious identity and commitment, are breaking down. Theorists now talk in terms of 'new syntheses of "hybridity", "collage", "solidarity" and so on'.[24] Things once held in total opposition now are seen as mutually enriching polar opposites. The context of theological debate is not what it used to be, a fact that destabilizes those who hitherto have comfortably resided in either the "evangelical" and "liberal" camps.

A holistic mission in contemporary society will attend not only to proclaiming the way in which God in Jesus has accepted sinners and liberated them to be open to the call placed upon their lives by others; it will also find us, for example, passionately campaigning on environmental issues, being committed to *Making Poverty History* and promoting peace-making practices. Out of a genuine appreciation of what is involved in Christian fellowship, we ought to rise above the practice of un-churching those whose emphasis falls in a different direction to the one we find congenial and affirming. We need one another to display a full exhibition of the gospel!

D. Key Areas for Attention

The burden of my message is simply this: if the contemporary church possesses a lively view of God, a positive attitude towards change, a critical approach to tradition, a relational view of society, a realistic understanding of church and a fundamental commitment to persons and the universe which sustains them, then people will encounter in it the true church. A church which intends to encounter others with the gospel will need to operate with something like the framework I have mentioned if it wants to connect with contemporary men and women and be faithful to the agenda of Jesus.

But what are the key areas to which this framework needs applying? Part of an honest answer to this question involves the painful recognition that a great deal of what we get up to in church life is largely beside the point of our calling to be a sign, expression and foretaste of God's reign of love over all things. It seems that we sometimes lose sight of what the institution is here for in our fervent work to keep the institution going. What I want to see in every local church is a radical commitment and honest attempt to review church life in the kind of spirit which would be generated if serious attention is given to my proposed

---

[24]   Lipner, "Religion and Religious Thinking in the New Millennium", p 87.

framework. Particular attention might be given to one specific early example of church life: 'They devoted themselves to the apostles teaching and fellowship, to the breaking of bread and the prayers'.[25] The early Jerusalem church is recorded as paying particular attention to teaching, fellowship and worship. That in turn became the driving force behind its proclamation of the gospel to others. Nothing could be more basic or vital: *teaching* - people becoming steeped in the doctrines and traditions of the lifetime of Christianity; *fellowship* – people experiencing the richness of a Spirit-filled community which is inclusive and committed to the welfare of those for whom Christ died; *worship* – the offering in words and song, reflection and silence, of all that is of our best to God; and thus *proclamation* – both inside and outside the church giving of an account of the hope that is within us.

There is not much future for churches with dispirited outlooks who are held captive to traditionalist attitudes. Their useful life is over, unless they re-discover a new vision for a fresh age. But there are enough quality people in our churches to lead the venture I'm calling for – a search within each local church for what God has for it to do today. Make teaching, fellowship and worship your key areas for consideration. Come at them on the basis of the kind of framework I've suggested and then be prepared for God to do exciting things with you!

---

[25]   Acts 2: 42.

CHAPTER FOUR

THE CORE ACTIVITIES OF THE ENCOUNTERING CHURCH: Lessons from the Jerusalem Church

A. COUNTER-CULTURAL CHURCH

(i) An Early Example of a Counter-Cultural Church

What we know about the early Jerusalem church, arguably the first Christian congregation, is largely derived from the Acts of the Apostles. There we find three brief summaries of its life.

> They devoted themselves to the apostles' teaching and fellowship, to the breaking of bread and the prayers.
> Awe came upon everyone, because many wonders and signs were being done by the apostles. All who believed were together and had all things in common; they would sell their possessions and goods and distribute the proceeds to all, as any had need. Day by day, as they spent much time together in the temple, they broke bread at home and ate their food with glad and generous hearts, praising God and having the goodwill of all the people. And day by day the Lord added to their number those who were being saved.
> *Acts 2: 42-47*
>
> Now the whole group of those who believed were of one heart and soul, and no one claimed private ownership of any possessions, but everything they owned was held in common. With great power the apostles gave their testimony to the resurrection of the Lord Jesus, and great grace was upon them all. There was not a needy person among them, for as many as owned lands or houses sold them and brought the proceeds of what was sold. They laid it at the apostles' feet, and it was distributed to each as any had need.
> *Acts 4: 32-35*
>
> Now many signs and wonders were done among the people through the apostles. And they were all together in Solomon's Portico. None of the rest dared to join them, but the people held them in high esteem. Yet more than ever believers were added to the Lord, great numbers of both men and women, so that they even carried out the sick into the streets, and laid them on cots and mats, in order that Peter's shadow might fall on some of them as he came by. A great number of people would also gather from the towns around Jerusalem, bringing the sick and those tormented by unclean spirits, and they were all cured.
> *Acts 5: 12-16*

Luke's three short accounts of the Jerusalem church's life are extremely stylized. They are unlike any other account of church life in the New Testament. Whereas Paul's correspondence with the Corinthian church leaves us in no doubt about acute faults and failings in that congregation, everything appears well in the Acts account. The Seer of Patmos in Revelation writes about seven churches which have clear weaknesses that he points out quite sharply, but Luke paints an almost idyllic picture of the Jerusalem congregation: growing inexorably, perfectly attuned to the leadership of the Holy Spirit and united in perfect agreement. We have a clear choice concerning how we read Luke's summaries. Either we succumb to what might be called hermeneutical naivety by treating them at face value, thus accepting that there was once a church on earth unlike all the others we have known, or we adopt the strategy of hermeneutical suspicion, reading between the lines and acknowledging that the accounts are not fully reliable from a historical point of view. It is the latter strategy that most exegetes follow. Indeed, when the Act's account of the early Christian mission contradicts what we learn about it from Paul's letters, it is generally assumed that the Acts account is historically unreliable.

In short, we are wise to take what we read in these accounts with the proverbial pinch of salt. It is not very helpful to use them as perfect models that contemporary churches should copy. Times change and ways of being church in first century Jerusalem are unlikely to have been fully appropriate in Byzantium let alone in the contemporary West. Indeed, even Luke lets his halo slip when, amidst his overall theme of 'nothing can stop the gospel', he has to compromise his "everything they owned was held in common" claim (Acts 2: 44; 4:32). Not everyone was as good as Barnabas who sold his field and put the money in the common fund. There was also in this congregation the likes of Ananias and Sapphira who held some of their money back (Acts 4: 36 – 5:11). We all know what happened to Ananias and Sapphira – for doing what we do every time the offering plate comes round. [Given human nature it is hardly surprising that common ownership of property and wealth never caught on in the church, save among isolated small sects.] My point is simply this: the Jerusalem church was not as idyllic as Luke sometimes makes it out to be. All churches this side of eternity will have their problems, so if your congregation drives you mad to the point of distraction do not worry because that is par for the course as far as the church is concerned. Every church is a clay jar (2 Corinthians 4: 7); it is when churches pretend otherwise that they become menaces to the Kingdom.

Amidst this note of hard-headed realism about churches what can we glean of interest from these texts? First, the Jerusalem congregation was not an independent church like those to whom Paul addressed his letters or the Seer of Patmos critiqued in *Revelation*. It was largely a sect of Judaism. The Temple continued to figure prominently in the lives of its members (Acts 2: 46; 5: 12) and Jewish prayers were central to their devotional life (Acts 2: 42). If the term 'Christian' meant anything at all in this church, it certainly presupposed that one was Jewish. We cannot doubt, secondly, that good things were happening around the members. A healing ministry was taking place (Acts 2: 4; 5: 15-16). It was so effective that, not surprisingly, the church members were highly thought of in the wider Jewish community (Acts 5: 13). And, thirdly, the congregation was growing (Acts 2: 41, 47). If it had not, arguably, there would be no Christianity today.

Through their proclamation, activities and presence a growing group within Judaism were starting to offer an alternative view of reality and a different way of living. We should not over-estimate the alternatives and differences because initially Jewish outlook and practice certainly would have prevailed, but what had started was a process which led to a counter-culture, a body of people believing they were called to be different, and a community offering others a message about the meaning of existence and a way of living that was challengingly distinctive. Not surprisingly some members of the Jewish community recognized the subversive nature of the Jerusalem church members. "None of the rest dared to join them" (Acts 5: 13). Would that people today were staying away from the church because they feared the implications of what was involved, namely, a challenge to the prevailing world view, and hence the institutions that underpin it! And the more the first Christians attended to the essential activities at the heart of their community life, the more counter-cultural they became.

The contemporary church has become so wedded to contemporary culture that we often do not possess thought or practice different enough to really make a difference to people's lives. We have difficulty addressing a multi-faith world because our members do not seem to know what they believe or stand for as Christians, or, if they do, they possess little compulsion to share it with others. A parable of Jesus reminds us that: "The kingdom of heaven is like treasure hidden in a field, which someone found and hid; then in his joy he goes and sells all that he has and buys that field" (Matthew 13: 44). The indictment laid upon us is that sometimes we do not seem to value the treasure highly enough either to buy the field or even want to dig it up in the first place. Nor will we unless we attend to the basics of Christian discipleship.

The fourth thing of interest in Luke's stylistic summaries of the Jerusalem church concerns where the church members placed their emphasis in their church life. This reminds us of what we should be focussing on today: "They devoted themselves to the apostles' teaching and fellowship, to the breaking of bread and the prayers" (Acts 2: 42). Put bluntly, this teaches us that churches discover their distinctiveness when they attend to teaching, fellowship and worship. These three core activities are the driving force of an encountering church. They produce a people who make a difference to people's lives because they are different to the prevailing 'spirit of an age' (*zeitgeist*).

(ii) The Culture of Individualism

The prevailing world-view of the West is a distortion, perhaps even a mutation, of a belief which is profoundly Christian, namely, an individual's right to full personhood. Who we are must be allowed to flourish; no one individual or group should be allowed to make us what we are not called to be. The value that the contemporary Western world places upon human autonomy finds it origins in largely Christian attempts to set people free from constraints which diminish them: illiteracy, slavery, disease, racism, sexism, poverty and so on. Part of the church's response to Jesus' calling to bring life in its abundance to people has been found in its promotion of the quest for human self-determination (John 10: 10). It is only in relatively recent times that some people have been set free to lead their own lives; the vast majority in the world, however, remain held captive and oppressed. Hence we should be wary of damning a culture which champions the individual and sets out to allow me to be 'me', rather than defined by 'us' or, as is more usually the case, 'them'.

Nevertheless, there is a world of difference between the quest for true individuality and what has emerged from it, namely, the culture of individualism which so envelops our society. Today's seemingly 'me, myself and I' culture extols the virtue of 'the self-made man' (and, to be inclusive, 'the self-made woman'). In all our extolling of the virtues of competition we hardly ever hear people discussing the implications of the obvious fact that it is of the very nature of competitions that there are losers. It is fully realised that supposedly benign self-interest almost invariably promotes degrees of selfishness that exclude others from full participation in society. There is a childishness around in even the most sophisticated circles which fails to take into account Paul's universally valid law: ". . . when I want to do what is good, evil lies close at hand" (Romans 7: 21). The idea that wealth creation encourages generosity and charity may have some examples to support it, but there are other examples which can be lined up to negate it. The only thing assured about 'trickle-down' theories of wealth sharing is that the world's poor must think that the West has been living in permanent drought for much of the time.

The notion that the world ends with 'me', and that it is a basic human right that, within certain narrow limits, 'I' can do what I like with 'my' money or 'my' land, is all around us. It dominates politics, an arena now in which no political party can afford to extol the virtue of taxation. It is endemic in developing patterns of family life where the pursuit of individual satisfaction largely is starting to overtake our reciprocal responsibilities within marriage. The mushrooming of care-homes indicates not only the aging nature of our population but also our determination not to let our responsibilities to those who brought us here interferes with our individual aspirations. The culture of individualism underpins our attitudes to the environment which for many years seem to have revolved around the maxim that 'if it's there use it, exploit it, and make money out of it'. The more the ideology of individualism holds sway, the less fulfilled we seem to become. Consumerism is addictive: the more we get, the more we want – even to the point of going to dubious lengths to get it. A society which holds it to be the highest virtue that we look after number one results in two things: a residue of people who are unable for understandable reasons to be members of such a society, for example, the ageing or differently-abled and a lot of lonely people. Exclusion is the inevitable by-product of viewing persons largely in mechanistic terms related to production and output.

Increasing numbers of people are recognising this culture for what it is – profoundly deficient. Since time in memorial, and everywhere other than the contemporary West, people have recognised that life is centred not upon the individual but upon persons who exist in relation to other persons and the environment which sustains them. It may well be the case that competitiveness is built into the evolutionary framework of the universe, but so too is symbiosis, the ability for different species to co-exist for mutual benefit. We may well want to encourage individuals to work to the highest standard of their ability, but we would be foolish to ignore the truth of synergy – that the fruit of collaboration is greater than the collective energies of the participants. Nor should we ignore the value of diversity held within shared visions, as opposed to Cold War stand offs or competitive feuding. 'I am', not because 'I am an individual' but because 'I am related'. As Martin Buber says: "The word 'I' remains the shibboleth of humanity"[26] Yet we have foolishly made the individual into a god.

Outside the West and before the modern Western era people have believed that life is lived in relation to others, where 'others' usually included eternal Beings beyond the temporal world. It was inevitable that the culture of individualism

---

26   Martin Buber, *I and Thou*, 3rd edn (Edinburgh: T & T Clark, 1970), pp 115, 119.

should spawn the idea that as the drive towards human autonomy raises people's need for religion the supposed illusory transcendent domain would evaporate That, though, has not happened. To be sure, the church does not influence the affairs of state as much as once was the case, while in a multi-faith society Christianity no longer holds sway as once before, but people are searching spiritually, possibly more than ever before in recent times. Given the depressing predictions of the 1960's secularization theorists, the current interest in spirituality is quite remarkable. The culture of individualism has not delivered the goods:

> . . . increasing numbers of people feel as if their entire lives are being spent dealing with trivia, and wonder if they will ever escape from the spiral of misery and dissatisfaction in which they feel they are enmeshed. At a time when we in the West have more possessions and labour-saving devices than our forebears could ever have imagined, we seem to have lost our souls, and people are dissatisfied with the way our own identities have become false and shallow, apparently without meaning beyond the immediate moment.[27]

One cannot help but re-call Jesus who said: "One does not live by bread alone . . ." (Matthew 4: 4 and Luke 4: 4).

Granted what was said earlier about the church having become so wedded to our individualistic one dimensional society, we can sense the truth in John Drane's further observation that "we seem to have ended up with a secular Church in a spiritual society."[28]   Far from being a counter-cultural community which is a sign and sacrament of the Mystery which alone can satisfy human needs and aspirations, our congregations are caught up in the ethos of a consumerist culture which strives for efficiency, calculability, predictability and control.[29] But, thankfully, God is somewhat oblivious to such constraints – even if some in the church are prepared to let the church be overrun by management consultants! Against the backcloth of current management theory, I can humbly report that our evolving creation suggests that God is hopelessly inefficient, that Christian assessments of value extend far beyond what can be measured or calculated, that the Holy Spirit is forever breaking the bounds of predictability, and that God works by giving people freedom rather than taking total control over their lives.

---

[27] John Drane, *The McDonaldization of the Church: Spirituality, Creativity, and the Future of the Church* (London: Darton, Longman and Todd Ltd), p 21.
[28] Ibid. p 54.
[29] See ibid. pp 34-54.

(iii) The Culture of Encounter

Martin Buber, Jewish theologian, philosopher and one of the great prophets of the twentieth century, saw clearly the danger of viewing people and the world in which they live as objects totally stripped of the relations which give them real value. There are times when it is important to be objective, to view from a distance and disengage. Science, of course, depends upon treating what is 'other' as an 'It'. So a tree becomes a piece of wood which can then be studied to determine its age or chemical composition or whatever. But a tree is more than merely an 'It', a subject for investigation or, even, fuel for burning. It is related to other trees, as well as being an essential part of the eco-system. Birds build their homes in it, insects get their food from it and we value its shade on a burning hot day. It is related – more than an 'It'; it becomes a 'You' to all who take it seriously. Buber argues, therefore, that the sentence 'I see the tree' is not fundamentally about my viewing something objectively, but rather it concerns a relation between an 'I' and a tree. The relation is primary, not the isolated individual.[30] In certain extreme cases we must treat 'things' as things, but more often than not we must view them in relation to us and other things if we are to do them justice. From holocaust to global warming, from slavery to agricultural chemicals, however, the world of 'I-It' has triumphed over the world of 'I-You'.[31] And the profundity of Buber's thought becomes apparent when he boldly asserts that ". . . in every You we address the eternal You".[32] When we enter into relations with the other as You, rather than treat what is other as merely an It, we not only discover the true other, but also that the other can become the means by which we relate to God. Indeed, the myriad of relationships which make up the universe find their beginning and end in the Eternal You, the living God. As Buber says:

> Only one You never ceases, in accordance with its nature to be You for us. To be sure, whoever knows God also knows God's remoteness and the agony of drought upon a frightened heart, but not the loss of presence. Only we are not always there.[33]

We may give up on God, but God does not give up on us; we may sever our side of the covenantal relationship, but God holds fast to God's side!

---

[30]   Buber, *I and Thou*, p 67.
[31]   Ibid. p 53.
[32]   Ibid. p 57.
[33]   Ibid. p 147.

Buber's thought has been very influential in Christian theology, not least because it so perceptively captures a central teaching of Jesus. We find our true selves, said Jesus, not in isolation from others but in relationships generated by love – our relationship with God and with all those whom God places a claim upon our lives (Mark 12: 28-34). The essence of abundant life is found in reciprocal relationships with God and our neighbours, and, as Jesus taught, it is in serving our neighbours that we end up meeting him (Matthew 25: 31-46). All those the society of his day treated as mere 'Its', for example, the women, children, lepers, tax-collectors and sinners beyond forgiveness, Jesus brought to the centre, treating them as precious 'Yous'. He challenges us now to refute the culture of individualism by replacing the individual at the centre of our world with God and neighbour. It is solely by virtue of our power to relate that we are able to live in the spirit.[34]

(iv) The challenge of being an Encountering Church

The Christian message is that, contrary to the ideology of individualism, true fulfilment comes from reciprocal relations with God and neighbours rather than through attempts at self-sufficiency. If this message is to be heard it will be as much through what we are as by what we say and do. Does our church life match what we proclaim? Many outside the church think not. They view us as judgemental rather than affirming, exclusive rather than inclusive, concerned with perpetuating the institutional trappings of Christianity rather than selfless service of our neighbours. By and large, and more and more, how we are church is not connecting with today's spiritual searchers. The task we now face is one of re-inventing ourselves so that we become an encountering church that makes a difference to people's lives. And, as I have argued, the necessary shape we need to be in if we are to become a faithful church will only emerge if we attend to the core activities we found present in the Jerusalem church. To a consideration of those we turn.

B. THE COVENANTING COMMUNITY OF THE FRIENDS OF JESUS

Let us remind ourselves of the text which refers to the Jerusalem church's core activities: "They devoted themselves to the apostles' teaching and fellowship, to the breaking of read and the prayers" (Acts 2: 42).

Albeit out of order, we begin with the word 'fellowship'. 'Fellowship' is one of the great biblical words. It points to a distinctive feature of the Christian counter-culture. "'See how these Christians love one another", it was said of the early

---

[34]   Ibid. p 89.

church.[35]   And whatever lies behind the word 'fellowship' it most certainly had something to do with those first 'gathered saints' re-presenting to the outside world the love of God which had drawn near to them in the life and ministry, death and resurrection of Jesus.[36] And yet, few biblical words have suffered as much dilution and devaluation through use. When I hear the world 'fellowship' banded around in church circles I often groan. What was meant by 'fellowship' in New Testament times was rather more than a cup of tea and a chat. Any group of human beings can have that kind of fellowship – down the pub, at the old folk's club or on the local rambling club excursion. Charles Cranfield notes "the newness and uniqueness" of the fellowship experienced by the early Christians, and he concludes that it involved "a *togetherness* for deeper than any mere camaraderie".[37] Let us begin with the biblical background of the word 'fellowship'.

(i) Biblical Background of *koinonia*

'Fellowship' translates the Greek world *koinonia*. In Classical Greek *koinonia* means an 'association' or 'partnership'. Used in its most far-reaching sense *koinonia* is simply another word for society, but when used more specifically of groups in society it points to "the spirit of generous sharing as contrasted with the spirit of selfish getting."[38] One immediately gets a sense of the way in which *koinonia* is a counter- cultural concept in an overtly individualistic culture. When the Greeks used *koinonia* they were pointing to "a close and intimate relationship into which people enter".[39] It was applied to business partnerships and marriage, but also significantly to a person's relationship with God.

In the Septuagint, the Greek translation of the Hebrew Scriptures, we find *koinonia* often translating the Hebrew word *chabar*. This helps us gain a little understanding of what the first Jewish Christians would have understood by 'fellowship'. More than a loose association of people would clearly have been in their minds since *chabar* means 'to bind or join together'. The word is used when speaking about joining curtains together (Exodus 26: 6), nations forming alliances (Genesis 14: 3), a house mutually shared (Proverbs 21: 9) and bands of fisherfolk

35   Tertullian in *Apology* 39 found in *The Ante-Nicene Fathers*, ed Alexander Roberts and James Donaldson (Grand Rapids, Michigan: Eerdmans, 1989).

36   Rodney Stark's *The Rise of Christianity* (Princeton, New Jersey: Princeton University Press, 1996 shows how a great deal of early conversations was the result of 'practical' Christianity which was rooted in the love command of Jesus.

37   Charles Cranfield in Alan Richardson ed., *A Theological Word Book of the Bible* (London: SCM Press, 1957) p 82.

38   William Barclay, *New Testament Words* (London: SCM Press, 1964), p 173.

39   Ibid.

(Job 41: 6). Interestingly *chabar* is hardly ever used in the Hebrew scriptures of a person's relationship with God out of reverence for the holiness of God. When it came to God, tradition suggested that one kept one's distance. (See 2 Samual 6: 1-11. In Deuteronomy 12: 7, 12, 18 the Israelites enjoy "the presence of the Lord" but stand "before the Lord" thus emphasising a reverent distance). This implies that, God's coming in Jesus not withstanding, the early Jewish Christians would not have understood fellowship in any cheap sense. Over-familiarity with God would not have been acceptable since their cultural background necessitated speaking of their relationship with God in ways which recognized the distance and inequality there is between God and persons. Equally, our Christian awareness of being indebted to God's grace should warn us also against being over-familiar with God.

But what can we lean from the use of *koinonia* (and cognate words) in the New Testament? What did the early church mean by the word which translates as 'fellowship'?[40] First, the early Christians used *koinonia* to refer to a sharing of friendship based upon them becoming the friends of God through Jesus (1 John 1: 3). Symbolically, this friendship was expressed, for example, through sharing 'the right hand of fellowship' (Galatians 2: 9). Secondly, *koinonia* expressed the way in which the early Christians had graciously been given a share in all that flowed from the life, death and resurrection of Christ. Through the Christ event they had received a share of God's grace (Philippians 1: 7), of the gospel (2 Corinthians 9: 13; Philippians 1: 5), of the promise (Ephesians 3: 6), of the final glory (1 Peter 5: 1), of the body and blood of Christ at the Lord's Table (1 Corinthians 10: 16), of the Holy Spirit (Philippians 2: 1) and even of God (1 John 1: 3, 6; 2 Peter 1: 4). Thirdly, *koinonia* involved early Christian participation in the suffering of Christ (Philippians 3: 10). The first Christians trod the way of Christ in cross-bearing allegiance – hence their stress on martyrdom when the church underwent persecution. Membership of the church was at a price, usually marginalization and very often the ultimate sacrifice. Grace didn't come cheap. And fourthly, the early church understanding of *koinonia* pointed to an integrated and holistic sense of Christian mission. The churches were generous because God in Christ had been generous to them. A collection was arranged among the churches to help the needy in the mother church in Jerusalem; it established ecumenical fellowship between Jewish and Gentile churches. Deacons were set apart in the Jerusalem church to serve the congregation in response to the servanthood of Christ (Romans 15: 26; 2 Corinthians 8: 4; 2 Corinthians 9: 13).

---

[40] A great deal of this section is indebted to the writings of Charles Cranfield and William Barclay in the books cited above at n12 and n13.

The love, sense of unity and mutual care which was evident among and beyond the church membership was earthed in a powerful awareness of its origin being rooted in and flowing from God's generosity. Their worship of God and their concern for their neighbour were integrated; piety went hand in hand with politics; sacrament led to service.

(ii) Reclaiming the Tradition of 'Covenant'

The richness of what lies behind the idea of Christian fellowship is coming into view. More treasures are to be discovered if we reclaim part of our heritage. What marked out our forebears in English Dissent was that they were not only 'separatists' but also 'covenanters'. They 'separated' from the Church of England, protesting about the monarch's dictate that they should limit their worship to the Prayer Book. As Protestants and Dissenters, though, they covenanted together to establish churches in the biblical belief that the church is constituted 'where two or three' gather in the name of Christ (Matthew 18: 20) – not only where there happens to be ordained ministers, and particularly not where those ministers happen to be loyal to the Crown! What they understood as Christian 'fellowship' was actually largely governed by their understanding of 'covenant'. We are reminded that there is more to 'fellowship' than simply an association of people.

The term 'covenant' spans the entire Bible.[41] In the Hebrew Scriptures, God makes a covenant with Abraham (Genesis 17: 2). In spite of human sin and recalcitrance, God constantly is found re-affirming that Covenant. Meanwhile, at pivotal moments in Israel's history, God acts within the covenantal relationship: the giving of the Ten Commandments (Exodus 19: 5-20: 17), the spiritual pilgrimage of Jeremiah which culminates in the so-called 'inner covenant' (Jeremiah 31: 31-34), and the Exile during which the Israelites are told they must become a covenant to the rest of the world (Isaiah 42: 6). Then, in the history of the church, we find the theme re-appearing: Jesus at the Last Supper re-enforces Jeremiah's idea of 'inner covenant' when he announces, 'This is my body . . . . This is the New Covenant in my blood' (Mark 14: 22-25; 1 Corinthians 11: 23-26), while in the great vision of the New Jerusalem in *Revelation* we learn that at the End the covenant will remain:

See, the home of God is among mortals.
He will be with them as their God;
they will be his peoples,
and God himself will be with them . . .   (21: 3; cf Jerermiah 31: 33).

---

[41]   My understanding of 'covenant' owes everything to Edgar Jones, an Old Testament scholar who kindled my love for the Hebrew Scriptures.

But what can we learn about Christian fellowship from the concept of covenant so central to our forebears' ecclesiology? Five characteristics of 'covenant' collectively press home to us the counter-cultural ethos of the church.

a)   In Christian fellowship God takes the initiative. Central to the covenant motif is the fact that covenant is the unmerited gift of God. It was not earned or deserved by the Hebrews, but graciously given (Genesis 9: 17; 17: 7). On this basis Jesus also established Christian fellowship: "You did not choose me but I chose you" (John 15: 16). We are part of the Christian fellowship at God's invitation. *Koinonia* is a divine gift, not a human creation.

b)   Christian fellowship involves relationships between unequals. As I remember Edgar Jones thundering: "A covenant is not a contract!" The idea that God and the Hebrews entered into a contract of mutual benefit is foreign to the Bible. The Hebrew word for covenant (*berith*) is used of table-fellowship that the strong offer the weak. In Christian fellowship, as in covenant, the strong contribute to the weak. The church is the home of the poor, oppressed, stranger and alien. Membership of the covenanting community carries obligations to others.

c)   Christianity is born out of participation in a community. While there are a few references in the Hebrew scriptures to God making a covenant with key individuals (2 Samual 23: 5; Psalms 89: 3, 28), the motif of covenant is firmly set in a community context. God does not make private treaties. Though God treats us as persons, person-hood can only be fleshed out fully in community (Jeremiah 32: 36-40). The covenant idea leaves no room for the solitary Christian.

d)   Christian faith engages the whole person. A striking feature of the deepening theology of the Hebrews in scripture is their passage from dependence upon the written laws of the Ten Commandments to their reliance upon the inner covenant of Jeremiah: "But this is the covenant that I will make with the house of Israel after those days, says the Lord: I will put my law within them, and I will write it on their hearts; and I will be their God, and they shall be my people" (Jeremiah 31: 33). The Hebraic-Christian tradition reaches its height in the recognition that what ultimately matters is the commitment of our whole selves to God rather than obedience to a set of eternal rules.

e)   Christian fellowship leads to mission. The purpose of God's covenant with Israel was that Israel would be 'a light to the nations' (Isaiah 42: 6). The inner urge of mission was contained in the call of Abraham (Genesis 17: 1-3). God's people are chosen for service not privilege. Covenant entails mission.

We are accustomed to using the motif of 'covenant' in our ecumenical discussions, but given the plurality exhibited in many of our congregations it has a more local congregational use. It became the means by which our forebears understood being church, explaining why they came together in fellowship and pointing out what they were called to do. It was also the principal that governed their idea of church governance – members of the covenant gathered together to seek the mind of Christ. More akin to Quaker Meeting than the House of Commons, the background of the Church Meeting is rooted not only in the personal obligations of covenant members but also in a patient expectancy of waiting on God. 'Covenant' was the means by which diverse people were brought together in unity.

(iii) The Friends of Jesus

Friendship, says Sallie McFague, is "an unplumbed mystery we believe we understand until we begin thinking about it seriously".[42] And think about it seriously she does. Much of what follows I have learned from her. She helped me rescue the concept of 'friendship' from the rubbish-bin of the romantic novel and popular sentimentality. Indeed, the more I have reflected upon the matter, the more 'friendship' has opened up my understanding of church membership in important ways.

Friends are not related to us out of duty or function: we choose them and they choose us. Again we hear echoes of the great theme of covenant. Friendship not only involves mutual choice but also reciprocal relationships. As McFague puts it: "Friendship . . . is a joyful, free attraction between two people: a friend is someone you like and someone who likes you."[43] There are three paradoxes involved in such a relationship. First, although friendship is based upon a freely entered relationship, one of the strongest forms of bonding occurs: trust. This involves a commitment to stay loyal to one another and a common vision. Likewise the friends of Jesus freely choose to be members of the church, as McFague expresses the matter, "out of a sense of joy . . . join with God the friend in a mutual project of great interest to both: the well-being of the world."[44]

---

[42]   Sallie McFague, *Models of God: Theology for an Ecological, Nuclear Age* (London: SCM Press, 1987) p 58.
[43]   Ibid. p 160.
[44]   Ibid. p 163.

A second paradox emerges when we note that friendship between people implies an inclusive element. The common vision, in our case the Christian vision shared by church members, does not necessarily involve similar minds. Like-mindedness may have its attractiveness, but far more interesting, if more unpredictable and risky, is diversity. The friends of Jesus are not only numerous but also different: equality, race and gender do not come into play. In the church we have also to realize that there is no limit to the different people we will encounter as friends of Jesus. Jesus modelled this for us in the egalitarian nature of his acquaintances. He was dubbed "friend of tax collectors and sinners" (Matthew 11: 19) and told his disciples that they were no longer servants but friends (John 15: 12-15). ". . . Jesus' invitation to the outsiders to join him as friends at the table became an enacted parable of God's friendship with humanity: the God of Jesus is the One who invites us to table to eat together as friends".[45]

The third paradox concerns the way in which through friendship we discover ourselves in relation to the other. There is a mutuality and reciprocity involved in friendship which helps us recognize that we are interdependent creatures. We may feel that we choose to be in relation with the other, but in fact a radical inter-relatedness of some kind undergirds our every moment. As McFague says: " . . . from the cells of our bodies to the greatest visions we hold in common, relationship and inter-relationship are at the heart of our existence."[46] Friendship may sound a very childish concept, but actually it is a very radical idea. True autonomy is found not as many adults think in individualism but as children know instinctively in relationships. When this is experienced from a Christian perspective we speak of our relatedness to God and neighbour. Life in the church, therefore, should be an example to society of what community involves. It ought to say: 'We do not belong to ourselves; there are friends who have a claim on our lives. Nor are we left to ourselves, there are friends, as well as God, who care for us.'

It follows that central to the ethos of the friends of Jesus is hospitality. The starting point for understanding hospitality is the inclusivily of Jesus' table fellowship and particularly his invitation at the Last Supper. "The shared meal that satisfies the body and delights the spirit, the meal to which all are invited, including both human and nonhuman outcasts, is the metaphor for the community established by God as friend."[47] The Christian community therefore must be open enough to include strangers as friends. *Koinonia* includes not just the like-minded but all human beings. When we take the world we inhabit seriously, it also in a

---

[45]   Ibid. p 168.
[46]   Ibid. p 167.
[47]   Ibid. pp 172-173.

profound sense includes the whole of life. Now is the time to affirm this, in this age of xenophobia, occasioned by fears over those the Bible calls 'strangers and aliens' and then challenges us to make our friends, in this time of post 9/11 fear when what some seem more than willing to die for, namely, the 'outsider', is not necessarily an enemy but simply a stranger; in this era of global warming when we must realize that friendship needs extending to the earth.

C. HOLISTIC WORSHIP

*A*cts 2: 42 informs us that the early Jerusalem church devoted itself not only to 'fellowship' but also to 'the breaking of bread and the prayers'. It would appear, therefore, that the worship pattern of this congregation was partly old and partly new, following Jewish traditions and yet being innovative. Let us first of all attend to the innovation.

(i) The Centrality of 'The Breaking of Bread'

The Jerusalem church remained Jewish, but with the rather distinctive addition of what is called 'the breaking of bread'. This was an activity distinct from sharing meals together as a fellowship, even if hardly ever separate from communal eating. ". . . they broke bread at home and ate their food with glad and generous hearts" (Acts 2: 46). We can conclude that while their public worship was Jewish, in the privacy of their homes and when they joined together at communal meals, *the* distinctive feature of Christian worship was emerging, 'the breaking of bread'.

To be sure, the distinctive feature of Jerusalem church worship was not yet the Sacrament of Holy Communion as we know it; it was more 'agape' than 'Eucharist'. But what is referred to as 'the breaking of bread' was this particular early church's attempt to follow the command of Jesus to "do this is remembrance of me" (Luke 22: 19; 1 Corinthians 11: 24). We get a further picture of another church's effort to follow this command in Paul's correspondence with the Corinthians. There we find a church, at a slightly later time and in a very different culture, failing to follow faithfully what Paul refers to as the tradition "I received from the Lord" and "handed on to you" (1 Corinthians 11: 23). Two things are beyond argument: first, 'the breaking of the bread' lay at the heart of early church worship, and, secondly, there were debates and arguments about the format it should take. At one and the same time, what we have come to know as 'the sacrament of Holy Communion', 'the Lord's Supper', 'Eucharist' or 'Mass' has anchored churches in a common heritage as well as being a matter of contention and division between them. The very basis of the church's unity, the celebration of the life laid down for all, has been the battleground upon which feuding groups of Christians have taken sides.

It is surprising how often in Christian history the distinctive feature of Christian worship has been marginalised in ecclesiastical practice. The Lord's Supper sometimes has not featured highly in the worshipping life of the average believer. For example, in the Mediaeval church worshippers observed the sacrament rather than participated in the celebration. Communion became a distant rite conducted by priests and hence developed all kinds of magical connotations. And, of course, if part of the magic was that eating consecrated bread and drinking consecrated wine set one free from the consequences of one's sin, it made sense to do this when the possibility of committing further sins post-participation was reduced to a minimum. The tradition of taking communion once at the very end of one's life on one's death-bed consequently was very common. Another example of the marginalisation of the Lord's Supper comes from the Church of England. The major service in the Church of England today is 'parish communion', but when I was a boy it was matins. In fact, it is only recently that Anglicans have taken Holy Communion on a regular, weekly basis. The previously normative frequency of participation was once a year on Easter Sunday – a fact that some younger Anglicans will find rather surprising. And for a third example, we come nearer to home. In the Free Church world, preaching often became so elevated in importance that the Lord's Table was eclipsed. We can see this from patterns of architecture. Large central pulpits tower over Communion Tables whose primary purpose seems to have been the location of the church flowers. Word and Sacrament were torn apart, with the celebration of the Lord's Supper being tagged on to the main preaching service as a separate service, from which large numbers absented themselves. Thankfully, only the last vestiges of that practice remain: the occasional communion collection during the last hymn, or what lay behind the request made to me quite recently that I pause at the end of the pre-communion hymn since "there are one or two who like to leave after the sermon".

In the traditions of the United Reformed Church we find diversity in the frequency of communion practice: Presbyterian quarterly, Congregational monthly and Churches of Christ weekly. All the evidence points towards increasing frequency of participation in the Lord's Supper in our churches, sometimes under the encouraging influence of ecumenical partners. I am not alone in thinking that we should not deprive those who feel the need for weekly communion from having it. One of the virtues of post-modern society is an acceptance that diverse needs should be met since people are different. Unity therefore does not always mean everyone all doing the same things together, but is all about belonging to a community which ensures that different needs are met in appropriate ways. The debate in Church Meeting should centre on the worship needs of the many different people who make up, or might want to become part of. the church membership. At present it tends to result in the lowest common denominator of acceptability. But God sometimes asks us to do things for others that we do not want for ourselves. David Jenkins, therefore, provides a challenge for us in his memorable words: "I cannot be fully me until you are fully you, and that means that you must be you in such a way that it enables me to be me; and similarly I must be me in such a way that it enables you to be you."[48] We have to create patterns of worship which meet the needs of different ages, temperaments and tastes. Given the limited resources of the average congregation this can only be done ecumenically.

Giving renewed attention to 'the breaking of bread' is very apposite in our contemporary culture, governed as it largely is by visual images. Indeed, the genius of Jesus in his instruction to 'do this in remembrance of me' lies in his placing a holistic activity central. The Lord's Supper appeals to all the senses and can be appreciated at many different levels. At the table, young and old, intellectual and artist, dramatist and poet, find different ways to experience the Mystery that is the power, presence and promise of God's love. A lot of Reformed worship, however, fails to connect with many people because, by nature, it can become the privileged preserve of cerebral people. Words dominate; preaching often underplaying what can be grasped by sight or experienced through the emotions. It is very significant that World War I chaplains often found their words empty but the Sacrament of Holy Communion powerful as they ministered to people in difficult days. But these days are also difficult days, and people are no different to then. Equally important is the way in which the drama of the Lord's Supper connects with those whose make-up renders them most open to insight through visual and experiential media, or whose understanding is limited due to age or disability. Given the centrality of 'the breaking of bread' in the early church, it remains somewhat of a mystery why churches which owe so much to the thinking of John Calvin never took up his insistence upon holding together 'Word' and 'Sacrament' in a weekly service. But, then, as in other things, Presbyterians and Congregationalists were and often are a law unto themselves. Just what Calvin would have made of our individual communion glasses and cubes of bread we can only guess – I suspect it would have rendered him speechless, as it should anyone who attends to the symbolism of the Eucharistic drama of the breaking of bread and sharing of the cup!

---

[48]   David E. Jenkins, *God, Jesus and Life in the Spirit* (London: SCM Press, 1988), p 71.

We now turn to what is referred to as 'the prayers'. This refers no doubt to the prayers offered at the major religious festivals and particularly those that were used inside the family home. Their content is largely unknown, but it is reasonable to assume that *The Psalms* provides us with insights into Jewish people's praise at the time. And from those insights we can gain a great deal to enhance the content of contemporary Christian praise.

(ii) Worship Themes from the Psalms

The Psalter has often been referred to as 'the hymn-book of the Jewish church'. We can be pretty confident that it was predominant in the worship of the Jerusalem church mentioned in the *Acts of the Apostles* and it certainly was in use in the churches at Corinth (1 Corinthians 14: 26) and Ephesus (Ephesians 5: 19). Indeed, right up to the present, "public worship has continually created and cultivated a particular intimate relationship of the worshipping congregation to the psalms."[49] This is particularly true of the Reformed tradition, as the centrality of metrical psalm singing in some of our churches amply testifies. It is not an over-estimation to say that, when the church has wanted to explore the content of its worship, the Psalter has played an influential role in the ensuring exploration. So, in keeping with this tradition, what does a reading of the Psalms offer us by way of guidance concerning the themes which should be apparent in Christian worship today? I have located ten, though no doubt there are others.

(1) Reverence: A Sense of the Holy

Worship involves entering the presence of God, which, following the psalmist, is something that needs doing appropriately. This is not a fellowship of equals:

> To you I life up my eyes,
>   O you who are enthroned in the heavens!
> As the eyes of servants
>   look to the hand of their master,
> as the eyes of a maid
>   to the hand of her mistress,
> so our eyes look to the Lord our God,
>   until he has mercy upon us.
>
> (Psalms 123: 1-2)

---

[49]   Artur Weiser, *The Psalms: A Commentary* (London: SCM Press, 1962), p 19.

God is God and we are God's subjects: that must never be forgotten. It should lead to awe, what the Bible calls 'fear': ". . . the Lord takes pleasure in those who fear him, in those who hope in his steadfast love" (Psalms 147: 11). What we offer to God, therefore, must be fitting to God: "Let the words of my mouth and   the meditation of my heart be acceptable to you, O Lord, my rock and my redeemer" (Psalms 19: 14). It should respect God's holiness (Psalms 96: 9; 99: 3, 5). It is a time for listening to God and removing self from centre-stage: "For God alone my soul waits in silence" (Psalms 62: 1, 5). This is all a far cry from the predictability, staleness and even boredom which masquerades as 'reverence' in much of our worship.   Reverence involves active engagement, silences which are deafening and spaces left vacant for God to enter.

(2)   **Adoration: 'Wowed' by God's Grandeur**

The more we seek God and listen to God, the more our breath is taken away. It is appropriate that we contemplate God: "On the glorious splendour of your majesty, and on your wondrous works, I will meditate" (Psalms 145: 5), for that is the way to recognize God as God, avoiding the ways we trim God down to suit our sensibilities.   If ever there is a danger of our worship treating God with over-familiarity, we should read those Psalms that rigorously lay out the way in which Yahweh is like no other God (Psalms 104; 135; 136). Before Yahweh one cannot but fall down on one's knees.   This is a God like no other: Wow, worship and adore!

(3)   **Thanksgiving: Responding to God's Generosity**

Large sections of the Psalms are devoted to extensive accounts of what God has done for us. A beautiful example goes as follows:

> When I look at the heavens, the work of your fingers,
>   the moon and the stars that you have established;
> what are human beings that you are mindful of them,
>   mortals that you care for them?
>
> Yet you have made them a little lower than God,
>   and crowned them with glory and honour.
> (Psalms 8: 3-5)

We owe God everything; nothing we enjoy would have been possible without God. So ...

I will give thanks to the Lord with my whole heart;
I will tell of your wonderful deeds.
I will be glad and exult in you;
I will sing praise to your name, O most High.

(Psalms 9: 1-2)

God is our creator and sustainer. In response to this generosity it is fitting to give thanks (Psalms 100: 4). We sing to God because God has dealt "bountifully" with us (Psalms 13: 6). God judges with "equity" and guides the nations (Psalms 67: 4). Therefore, "O magnify the Lord with me, and let us exalt his name together" (Psalms 34: 3).

(4) Lamentation and Supplication: Turning to God when at our Wit's End

Israel's religion was hammered out on the anvil of trouble and suffering, the Exile being one of the pivotal moments. The Psalms reveal that Jewish spirit typified by the story of the rabbis in a Nazi concentration camp. They put God on trial for crimes against humanity, found God guilty, and then returned to their prayers. Honest worship sometimes finds us railing against God at the same time as we turn to God; at other times, we refrain from attributing blame and just turn to God. The Psalms reveal a whole host of reasons that prompt supplication: illness (Psalms 31: 9-10), captivity (Psalms 42), violence (Psalms 7: 1-2), loneliness (Psalms 25: 16), sinfulness (Psalms 38: 3-4, 18) and, perhaps, underlying all these, a fear of death and ending up in the shadowy existence of Sheol or the Pit (Psalms 28: 1). So the general cry goes out to God: "Here the voice of my supplication, as I cry to you for help, as I lift up my hands toward your most holy sanctuary" (Psalms 28: 2). Indeed, in Psalms 107 we hear of a lengthy catalogue of desperate conditions in which people found themselves. At the end of each description we read; "Then they cried out to the Lord in their trouble" (Psalms 107: 6, 13, 19, 28), and, of course, those words are quickly followed by "and [God] delivered them from their distress" (Psalms 107: 6). When sorely troubled, the psalmist presents the assurance of God: "Out of my distress I called upon the Lord; the Lord answered me and set me in a broad place" (Psalms 118: 5) and "I sought the Lord, and he answered me, and delivered me from all my fears" (Psalms 34: 4). A spirituality developed which says that if God has looked after our ancestors, so God will look after us. Hence, we have nothing to fear. It is a robust spirituality, one which needs to be at the heart of Christian worship.

(5)   **Offering: Placing Our Lives before God, Warts and All**

The Psalms quite often present a chilling portrait of the human condition:

> God looks down from heaven on humankind
>> to see if there are any who are wise,
>> who seek after God.
> They have all fallen away, they are all alike perverse;
>> there is no one who does good, no, not one.
>> (Psalms 53: 2-3)

We are sinners; our sin offends God's holiness; and thus we stand under God's judgement: "He will judge the world with righteousness and the peoples with equity" (Psalms 98: 9. See also Psalms 96:13b). Sin is not a popular idea in our culture. We often seek alternative explanations for our wrongdoing, sometimes totally transferring the blame from the individual to systemic forces like social upbringing or depravation. Every age, though, finds a way to pass the buck – Adam and Eve in Eden were but our prototypes! This is not to deny that systemic forces influence behaviour, only to observe that they do not totally determine it. Otherwise all poor people would be criminals and all the well-heeled virtuous. But that is not the case. With a conviction grounded upon a universal amount of supporting evidence, Paul asserted that he found it "to be a law that when [he wanted] to do what is good, evil lies close at hand" (Romans 7: 21). It follows that we all have something to confess; we are all sinners. It is interesting to note that years of listening to students conduct worship has thrown up the revealing fact that if any type of prayer is absent in the worship they construct it is usually the prayer of confession!

The psalmist took the human condition most seriously: we are sinners, so let us get things out into the open: "As for me, I said, 'O Lord, be gracious to me; heal me, for I have sinned against you'" (Psalms 41: 4). Once we are open about our faults and failings, we are at the mercy of a forgiving God. Those who think that ideas of forgiveness originate with the cross of Jesus, though, haven't read the Psalms thoroughly!

> Then I acknowledged my sin to you,
>> and I did not hide my iniquity;
> I said: "I will confess my transgressions to the Lord",
>> and you forgave the guilt of my sin.
>> (Psalms 32: 5)

> The Lord is merciful and gracious,
> > slow to anger and abounding in steadfast love.
> He will not always accuse,
> > nor will he keep his anger forever.
> He does not deal with us according to our sins,
> > nor repay us according to our iniquities.
>
> > > > > (Psalms 103: 8-10)

Absolution will follow confession in the experience of the faithful worshipper. While the Psalms leave us in no doubt how far human beings have 'fallen' from "the likeness of God", and therefore recognize the scale of the 'turning around' (*metanoia*) which is involved in any path to righteousness, they never forget that however great the scale of human wrong doing men and women remain in "the image of God" (Genesis 1: 26). Human worth ultimately is the gift of the creator; the gifts we possess are an out-working of being in the creator's image. And, yet, in Christian theology as well as in Christian worship, people have so often been viewed as totally worthless. Many has been the preacher who has felt constrained to bring people to their knees before attempting to lift them to heaven, only to leave their hearers in a quagmire of guilt and feeling utterly valueless. The Psalms offer more by way of theological balance.

The Psalms take sin seriously, but they also testify to the way in which being human must be affirmed, can be celebrated and should be respected. For example, in Psalms 139 we find this much loved affirmation of the psalmist's very being before God:

> For it was you who formed by inward parts;
> > you knit me together in my mother's womb.
> I praise you, for I am fearfully and wonderfully made.
> Wonderful are your works; that I know very well.
> My frame was not hidden from you,
> > when I was being made in secret,
> > intricately woven in the depths of the earth.
> Your eyes beheld my unformed substance.
> In your book were written all the days that were formed for me,
> > when none of them as yet existed.
> How weighty to me are your thoughts, O God!
> How vast is the sum of them!
> I try to count them – they are more than the sand;
> I come to the end – I am still with you.
>
> > > > > (Psalms 139: 13-18)

Or, again, when the psalmist invokes to God to "Guard me as the apple of the eye" his prayer only makes sense if it is true that he has the worth before God that is not being granted by those "deadly enemies who surround [him]" (Psalms 17: 8-9). Worship should celebrate our God-given worth, provide an opportunity to offer back to God our giftedness, and show us how, who, and what we are can be offered in the service of God and neighbour. It must also be a place of protest when we support those who have their humanness ignored, violated or destroyed. We are the community that remembers: "For the needy shall not always be forgotten, nor the hope of the poor perish for ever" (Psalms 9: 18). We are people of a liberating God: "'Because the poor are despoiled, because the needy groan, I will rise up,' says the Lord; 'I will place them in the safety for which they long'" (Psalms 12: 5).

Our worship therefore should reflect a realistic view of human beings: a recognition that we are born in 'the image of God' and, therefore, that in some ways human life can be affirmed, celebrated and must be respected, but also an acknowledgement that this side of becoming 'in the likeness of God' this world will forever be a school for sinners.

(6)   Recollection: Stories about God's Ways with People

The psalmists drew strength from the past when facing extreme situations like illness, oppression and violence. It is quite clear that one strategy employed for coping with the extremities of life was to say: "Well, if God was a liberating presence with our forebears, so he will be for us now". Hope was kindled as they told and re-told the stories of God's past dealings with them. There are psalms which are devoted to such story-telling (Psalms 44: 1-3; 74: 12-17; 104; 106; 114; 137), and, on occasions, the psalmist was not averse to reminding God gently to live up to the people's past experiences: "Be mindful of your mercy, O Lord, and of your steadfast love, for they have been of old" (Psalms 25: 6). "Look, Lord", the psalmist seems to be saying "if you restored the fortunes of Zion in the past, get on with doing it again"! (see Psalms 126). At other times the psalmist is less pushy and rather more faithful – even if the outcome hoped for is largely the same:

> I will recall to mind the deeds of the Lord;
> I will remember your wonders of old.
> I will meditate on all your work,
>   and muse on your mighty deeds.

> (Psalms 77: 11-12)

And so must we, for a central part of our worship involves refreshing our minds and hearts in our stories of faith, particularly the classical ones found in scripture. "Tell me the stories of Jesus" the old hymn extols. Well, yes, of course . . . but, hopefully, we can get the message without having to suffer the sentimental hymn!

(7) Learning: Open to Discovering God's Ways

The Psalms challenge the people to attend to the living instruction of God: the Torah. This is linked, of course, with their retelling the stories of faith.

> Give ear, O my people, to my teaching;
>   incline your ears to the words of my mouth.
> I will open my mouth in a parable;
> I will utter dark sayings from of old,
>   things that we have heard and known,
>   that our ancestors have told us.
> We will not hide them from their children;
>   we will tell to the coming generation
>   the glorious deeds of the Lord,
>   and his might,
>   and the wonders that he has done.
>
>   (Psalms 78: 1-4)

Particularly challenging, perhaps, is the emphasis of nurturing the young in the family religious traditions. God's Word is offered as a yardstick. "How can young people keep their way pure?", the psalmist asks. The answer is, "By guarding it according to your word" (Psalms 119: 9). What are we passing on to the next generation from our living tradition? When will we grasp the nettle and accept that in a multi-faith society it is not the task of secular educators to nurture the young in *our* faith. Their job is educational, not confessional. Nurturing the young in *our faith* is *our* business.

On occasions the psalmist presents an attitude to learning which should delight every Christian educationalist. "Teach me your way, O Lord, that I may walk in your truth; give me an undivided heart to revere your name" (Psalms 86: 11. See also Psalms 25: 4-5). And we find a confidence in the Torah that is breath-taking when compared with the way the average Christian has marginalized the Bible to a dusty shelf. "Your word is a lamp to my feet and a light to my path" (Psalms 119: 105) is a well-known line.

Equally familiar perhaps is the following:

> The law of the Lord is perfect, reviving the soul;
> the decrees of the Lord are sure, making wise the simple;
> the precepts of the Lord are right, rejoicing the heart;
> the commandment of the Lord is clear, enlightening the eyes;
> the fear of the Lord is pure, enduring forever;
> the ordinances of the Lord are true and righteous altogether.
> More to be desired are they then gold, even much fine gold;
> sweeter also than honey, and drippings of the honeycomb.
>
> (Psalms 19: 7-10)

Would that our people came to church with positive attitudes like that to scripture! It is crucial that we remain open to the fact that God is on hand to teach us:

> I will instruct you and teach you the way you should go;
> I will counsel you with my eye upon you.
> Do not be like a horse or a mule, without understanding,
> whose temper must be curbed with bit and bridle,
> else it will not stay near you.
>
> (Psalms 32: 8-9; See also Psalms 34: 11-14)

(8) **Appropriateness: Worship which reflects who God is.**

The Psalms provide evidence of a long and tortuous battle in Judaism concerning whether Yahweh wants sacrifice. A priestly tradition does not go totally un-represented:

> I will come into your house with burnt-offerings;
> I will pay you my vows,
>   those that my lips uttered and my mouth promised
>   when I was in trouble.
> I will offer to you burnt-offerings of fatlings,
>   with the smoke of the sacrifice of rams;
> I will make an offering of bulls and goats
>
> (Psalms 66: 13-15)

However, a more prophetic voice is heard:

> For you have no delight in sacrifice;
>   if I were to give a burnt-offering,
>   you would not be pleased.
> The sacrifice accepted to God is a broken spirit;
>   a broken and contrite heart, O God, you will not despise.
>
> (Psalms 51: 16-17)

> I will praise the name of God with a song;
> I will magnify him with thanksgiving.
> This will please the Lord more than an ox
>   or a bull with horns and hoofs.
>
> (Psalms 69: 30-31)

True religion is rooted in inward devotion rather than outward ceremony. So the questing we need to ask is: Do our acts of worship enable inward devotion for those who attend? Or are they mere outward ceremonies? Does our worship follow the fashion of the age, or does it nourish folk to fashion their age? Is God pleased with what we get up to?

(9)   Intercession: Getting Alongside Others in their Plight

The Psalms include many examples of individuals crying out to God in their need confident that their need will be met: "I cry aloud to the Lord, and he answers me from his holy hill" (Psalms 3: 4). The psalmist can petition God with confidence because God has been gracious in the past:

> Answer me when I call, O God of my right!
> You gave me room when I was in distress.
> Be gracious to me, and hear my prayer.
>
> (Psalms 4: 1)

God makes room, creates space and provides a broad land in which people can flourish. Here are themes to preach on to the stressed-out inhabitants of our society, but the roots of the Psalmist's angst are more obvious than the hidden urges placed upon people by a consumerist society:

Deliver me, O Lord, from evildoers;
>   protect me from those who are violent,
>   who plan evil things in their minds
>   and stir up wars continually . . .
Guard me, O Lord, from the hands of the wicked;
>   protect me from the violent who have planned my downfall.
The arrogant have hidden a trap for me,
>   and with cords they have spread a net,
>   along the road they have set snares for me.

(Psalms 140: 1-2, 4-5)

Though oppression was more obvious to the psalmist than it is for many of us today, it is still easy for us to identify with the psalmist's petitions on behalf of others, for we also know the kind of people mentioned by the Psalmist: the ill, poor, oppressed, destitute, victims of violence. If we do not know their names, we have seen their faces on television. The psalmist intercedes on their behalf, confident that God stands alongside such people: "The Lord is near to the broken-hearted, and saves the crushed in spirit" (Psalms 34: 18). God is "the fellow sufferer who understands".[50] When we pray for others, we are not trying to get God to intervene in their situation, but rather attempting to discern what God is already doing in that situation.

Central of course to biblical thinking is the fact that God "loves righteousness and justice" (Psalms 33: 5; see also Psalms 37: 28) and, therefore, that God favours the just and is offended by the unjust (Psalms 106: 3). The king is prayed for in the following terms:

> Give the king your justice, O God, and your righteousness
>   to a king's son.
> May he judge your people with righteousness,
>   and your poor with justice . . .
> May he defend the cause of the poor of the people,
>   give deliverance to the needy, and crush the oppressor.

(Psalms 72: 1-2, 4)

And just rulers are deemed virtuous (Psalms 99: 4). God looks "down from his holy height . . . to hear the groans of the prisoners, to set free those who were doomed to die" (Psalms 102: 19-20). God did not leave the Israelites in

---

50   Alfred North Whitehead, *Process and Reality: Corrected Edition*, eds. David Ray Griffin and Donald W. Sherburne (New York: The Free Press, 1978) p 351.

Egyptian captivity, nor were they left in Babylonian exile. "The Lord works vindication and justice for all who are oppressed" (Psalms 103: 6. See also Psalms 126: 5-6). But the psalmist's concerns extend beyond those unjustly held captive. It encompasses what has been called 'God preferential option for the poor'. The psalmist believed that the poor are given special attention by God (Psalms 69: 33; 72: 4; 140: 12). They are victims of grave injustice to which God takes exception (Psalms 107: 39-41). It makes chilling reading for Westerners: "In arrogance the wicked persecute the poor – let them be caught in the schemes they have devised" (Psalms 10: 2. See also Psalms 11: 5). Poverty is not the mistake of the poor, in the psalmist's opinion it is the result of systemic oppression by the rich. So a clarion call goes out:

> Give justice to the weak and the orphan;
> maintain the right of the lowly and destitute.
> Rescue the weak and the needy;
> deliver them from the hand of the wicked.
>
> (Psalms 82: 3-4)

Not only do the intercessions of the psalmist provide us with very hard words about the acquisition of wealth – as my Grandfather wisely said, "Eh, lad, tha' can't tak it with thee!" (Psalms 49: 16-20), but they also reveal the belief that God looks with favour upon those who take care of the poor (Psalms 41: 1-3; 112: 9).

(10) **Confidence: Taking Risks and Singing New Songs**

Reading the Psalms one cannot but help but sense a degree of confidence that is also disarming. In spite of everything we seem to be told, God knows all about where we are; we can be assured that God is with us in it all, so we are never alone. No wonder the psalmist could look up into the hills and, with disdain for all forms of nature worship, declare that his help did not come from the hills but from "the Lord who made heaven and earth" (Psalms 121: 2). With a confidence rooted in what Christians have sometimes called 'assurance' we can appreciate his thinking when he declares:

> You who live in the shelter of the Most High,
> who abide in the shadow of the Almighty,
> will say to the Lord, "My refuge and my fortress;
> my God, in whom I trust."

For he will deliver you from the share of the fowler
>   and from the deadly pestilence;
>   he will cover you with his pinions,
>   and under his wings you will find refuge;
>   his faithfulness is a shield and buckler.
> You will not fear the terror of the night,
>   or the arrow that flies by day,
>   or the pestilence that stalks in darkness,
>   or the destruction that wastes at noonday.

(Psalms 91: 1-6)

On the back of that kind of confidence, risks can be taken and innovations made. 'The dead hand of traditionalism' only besets those who have lost touch with that 'living voice of tradition' which alone can generate confidence. Only those confident in the ultimate sufficiency of God can sing new songs with conviction (Psalms 149: 1). The reason why so much of our worship is moribund stems partly from our lack of confidence in the One who really matters and partly from the way we transfer confidence in God to forms of worship we find comfortable and familiar. Worship then becomes the end, rather than the means to the end.

(iii) Forms of worship

Our exploration of the Psalms has provided us with an illuminating insight into the content of worship. That content can be expressed in many forms. It is not the 'form' which worship takes that should trouble us, but that's often the sum total of our discussions about worship. Good worship comes in many styles, some which will suit our personal dispositions more than others. Perhaps most of us are impoverished by simply getting stuck into one style or pattern of worship? Be that as it may, worship, whatever its genre, should be understood holistically. In saying this I am suggesting that our worship should include those emphases from the Psalms that we have just explored, but I also want to re-iterate that worship must attend to all our senses.

In some ways, my plea for patterns of worship which engage the whole person and not just their minds is made in response to the perceived need of those beyond the church who are searching spiritually. John Drane suggests that "many people [seem] to be looking for a way of exploring spirituality that would be community-based, as well as being tactile, sensual, visual, and embodied".[51] I suspect that such

---

[51]   Drane, *The McDonaldization of the Church*, p 16.

---

needs are not just the latest fads of a post-modern culture; rather they are ongoing needs of people everywhere. Perhaps such needs were met at Jerusalem when they met to break bread and say the prayers? What I am clear about is that we must strive for worship whose form and content is holistic.

D.　LEARNING CHURCH

The Jerusalem congregation devoted themselves to three core activities. We have already explored 'fellowship' and 'the breaking of bread and the prayers'. We now turn to the third: the apostles' teaching.

(i)　The Apostolic Succession

It is not insignificant that Luke places devotion to the apostles' teaching as the first core activity of the Jerusalem church. Without the apostles' teaching there would be no church. The apostles were those sent to share the Good News of Jesus Christ with others. Without them Christianity would not have got off the ground. So there is a great deal of truth in the point made by one of my teachers, namely, that to be a Christian one is either an apostle or a person who bears witness to Jesus *after* the apostles, where the word 'after', of course, carries more than chronological significance and actually points to our 'following' and 'succeeding' those who started the Christian faith tradition. Schubert Ogden then would eye-ball us and with a twinkle in his eye say something to the effect that "None of us is an apostle. This means, as a matter of basic logic, that we are all standing in the apostolic tradition. We do not make Christianity up; rather we receive it". Several points flow from this very fundamental observation.

First, the Jerusalem church placed a great deal of importance upon the eye-witness testimony the apostles provided. The significance of the apostles was that they were *there*, so it was natural that the Jerusalem Christians should want to attend to the apostle's teaching. That was also true in the other early churches. Paul, who counted as an apostle following His Damascus road encounter, believed that his authority came from being one of the apostles, and when the likes of Peter and Paul died what counted in the church was establishing that thinking and practice was congruent with apostolic thinking and practice. First this was established by the use of oral traditions which flowed from the apostles, with the later reference point becoming the scriptures. But the basic point to note is that the notion of apostolic succession stands in the way of us making Christianity up.

Now, of course, the phrase 'apostolic succession' raises the matter of bishops. That is inevitable but regrettable, since what is at stake here is not the means by which the church believes 'the living tradition' is handed on, whether it be episcopal or conciliar, so much as the recognition that the church exists by a tradition which has been handed on, such that, in respect to that tradition, we must recognize that in principle there are limits to our innovations. In practice, of course, all the great debates, not to mention some of the church's most vexed quarrels, have concerned the legitimacy of innovation, whether it has been about the role of women or the authority of scripture, the place of lay people or inclusive language, to raise some recent issues. The notion of a living tradition being handed on, of course, is central to the New Testament. The Greek word involved means 'to hand down, pass on, transmit, relate, teach' (*paradidomi*). It occurs in several places in the New Testament (Mark 7: 13; Acts 6: 14; I Corinthians 11: 23).

There are at least four ways in which something can be handed on. First, most obviously, there is *repetition*. We leave what we receive intact as we pass it on. This is rather more difficult to achieve than one might think, witness games of Chinese Whispers! But the need to keep the Faith intact was one of the reasons why the church's oral traditions about Jesus came to be written down and later incorporated in the canon of scripture. It remains a matter of debate among New Testament scholars about which sections of the gospel tradition reflect the results of a process of oral tradition in which the tradition developed and which, if any, take us via the earliest witnesses to what Jesus actually said and did. But it remains important that we try to measure what we say and do today as Christians against the early Jesus traditions. Otherwise Christianity is severed from its roots. That, of course, is easier to say than achieve with precision.

The second model by which we can understand the idea of handing on tradition is *translation*. We move what is said in one culture into the language of another culture, always intending to retain the essence of what is being handed on. However, as we know, things always get lost in translation and, hence, 'translation' is no more straight forward than 'repetition' when it comes to understanding the process of handing on traditions. Few of us are so imperialistic, though, to deny that some sort of translation exercise is needed if Christianity is to be shared, not only across cultures but even inside them. It is arguable that the greatest task facing the once Christian West is one of communicating Faith inside the West. This involves translating the Christian message into the cultural language of a non-Church going culture.

The third model comes from the organic realm. As we observe an acorn giving rise to a sapling and then an oak tree, we witness a complex process of development. John Henry Newman was one prominent theologian who argued that this organic model provides an accurate way to understand how the Christian tradition has got to where it is from where it began. It is a helpful model since it explains how continuity and change can be held together in the process of 'handing on'. We might like to contemplate a fourth model, largely derivative from the notion of development, one which stresses the element of change over that of continuity. *Mutation* is a common phenomenon in the evolutionary process. We may sometimes wonder whether certain manifestations of Christianity are less understandable products of the evolutionary development of the living tradition than mutations of it. Be that as it may, it is clear that in the eyes of many traditionalists what some regard as legitimate developments of the Christian traditions others regard as unacceptable mutations.

A dispassionate reading of Christian history shows all four models being represented in the way the tradition has been handed on: repetition, translation, development and mutation of what has been handed all have taken place. Sometimes this has happened sequentially, one age moving forwards on one model of understanding, another age favouring one of the others. But, if our contemporary church scene is anything to go by, there are different groups within the church who each display approaches which reflect one or other of the four models: the fundamentalist is the follower of the repetition model; the conservative wants anchorage in the earliest forms but recognises the need to translate, the liberal extols the developmental approach; while the free-thinker is happy with whatever mutation fits his or her particular group. This observations leads to a point about the contemporary ecumenical scene, namely, that the greatest divisions in the Western church today are due more to style of tradition and ethos than of denomination. How often I hear it said: "I'm closer to some Anglicans, Methodists or Roman Catholics than I am to some fellow members of the United Reformed Church".

The first feature of any 'learning church' will be to follow the Jerusalem practice of stepping inside the inherited tradition. For them this was simply a matter of attending to the apostle's teaching; for us more is involved because the tradition has moved on. However, we will be wise if we attend to the earliest witnesses with particular attention because, in however complex a way, to be a Christian today involves following them. Why complex? Well, sometimes we most closely follow people by departing from them, because that was the way they got to where they were! We need to remember that "religious learning always balances continuity with change, remembering with reconstructing, transmitting with transforming".[52]   In such leaning, the past interacts with the present, often to generate something quite new. That helps explain why in the New Testament itself we find extensive Christian diversity, since Christianity under the influence of Peter in Jerusalem was somewhat different to Christianity under the influence of Paul. The church's unity creaked due to this diversity. Today's church scene is remarkably similar to the first century, although we are rather more prone to baptise our own ecclesial whims as authentic versions of the tradition. We can hear Paul asking: "Has Christ been divided?"

(ii) The Church's Current Educational Task

I once heard an educationalist say that a school which doesn't possess an explicit educational programme always has a hidden one. I came across the same idea recently when reading Thomas R. Hawkins', *The Learning Church*. Hawkins says that "The church does not have an educational programme; it is one".[53] What are we teaching people by where we meet, what we do when we are together and who we are made up of? We have a hidden curriculum which counts for much more than we realise. A run down church building, a handful of merely elderly people or poor music in worship says so much to people that they leave before we get a chance to speak with them. They vote with their feet. Part of our mission is to get our houses in order so that we can 'do' mission.

Returning to the Acts account, the word that translates as 'teaching' became the title of an early Christian education guide. We do not know its author or when it was written, but it probably originated in an isolated Christian community somewhere in Syria. *The Didache*, as it is known, is a short early Christian manual on morals and Christian practice. It describes the behaviour expected of those belonging to a counter-culture. People could read it, discuss it and seek to follow what it recommends. It was needed if people were to be nurtured into ways of thinking and patterns of living which were different from those outside the Christian community. An important question for us to address is why such aids are now absent from our churches and what does that absence tell us about our approach to education?

A recent North East Oecumenical Course Summer School was on the theme of 'mission in a multi-faith society'. It was held in Birmingham and involved visits to various faith communities: Sikh, Muslim, Buddhist and Hindu. At the gurdwara,

---

52   Thomas R Hawkins, *The Learning Congregation: A New Version of Leadership* (Louisville: Kentucky: Westminster John Knox Press, 1997), p 17

53   Ibid. p 40.

mosque, pagoda and temple each faith was introduced to us by a member of the particular faith community concerned. It was a fairly standard educational event in the life of any ordinand these days. What particularly interests me about such visits is that from each place I come away impressed by the ability of the ordinary members of these religious communities to speak in accessible ways about their faith tradition. What is really important to us we readily talk about. In the course of visits to the gurdwara, mosque, pagoda and temple, I have discovered moving and talkative people! At the Sikh gurdwara the talk was given by a young British-Asian woman, a mechanical engineering student with a heavy Birmingham accent. She spoke movingly about her faith, describing its essentials enthusiastically and with endearing joy. She recognized that being Sikh made her different, not just from other religious people but particularly from those of Faith or none who are snared by the norms and values of Western individualism. She understood her faith counter-culturally, speaking about a different way of understanding personhood; presenting a different perspective on family values; portraying a different lifestyle. Where could I have found a young woman in my church to offer as good an account of Christianity? And where can I acquire literature about Christianity as good as some I took home from the various places of worship that week? We must wake up to the fact that we have to communicate: we need a curriculum which enables newcomers as well as members to learn about the distinctiveness of Christianity, not least because our hidden curriculum for several years now has been telling people that we are on our way out. It is not insignificant that the more I attempt to break down barriers through inter-faith dialogue the more I am thrown back upon examining the distinctiveness of my faith. Religions make a difference to people by making people different – exploring those differences, living with the differences, even celebrating that they exist, is to make pathways towards peace and harmony in the world.

There was a time when the 'learning church' in the shape of the monastery was the only place of learning in society. From our churches came our universities, and when we Dissenters were thrown out of our universities in England we created Academies to provide a rigorous education for a Nonconformist world and a tradition of learned ministry which matched the best that came from Rome or Canterbury, and even surpassed most of it. I do not need to rehearse the contribution made by the churches to our educational provision. What the church once did became the province of the state; education was secularised. If some of the current debates about RE in schools are anything to go by, many seem to be of the view that the Christian nurture of our children (the few we have connected with our churches) should take place in state schools – rather, or as well as, in Christian homes and in our churches. The most heated argument I ever heard about the necessity of Religious Assemblies in schools came from an Anglican vicar whose dour approach to worship actually made sure that all the families with children went to alternative churches! Our schools, of course, must teach the Fourth R, since religions and their traditions are not only fascinating but also essential for a full understanding of life. In a multi-cultural society, however, it is the religions themselves who are responsible for the nurture of their young. What is all too clear today is that the kind of religious education being offered to the young at the gurdwara, mosque or temple seems far more thorough and committed than most of what is on offer in our churches. It will be rightly said that this is hardly surprising when one takes into account the need of religious minorities to maintain identities in alien cultures, but let us not forget that the Western culture of individualism is as alien to the Christian as it is to the Sikh, Muslim, Buddhist or Hindu.

During the late 1950's and early 1960s a significant movement took place in our churches which led to the adoption of what we came to know as 'Family Church'. In an age when only one out of three families are of the nuclear variety once normative in the West, we may well be surprised at the ease with which some churches still continue to model 'church' on the 'family'. Be that as it may, what happened in our churches during the subsequent years has been the introduction of what we now know as 'all age worship', followed by educational classes for children and young people. The great merit in all this was the attempt to bring children more fully into the worshipping life of the church and we must never go back to the time when children were excluded. The changes, however, had the effect of significantly reducing the time available for Christian education of children and young people. A senior church member once put it to me: "I went from having an hour with my class to less than half an hour". Notwithstanding the merits of an integrated approach to worship and education, we might ask ourselves seriously whether we are giving sufficient attention to what was once known as catechetical education. Questions about whether Sunday is the right time and how best to make it attractive and exciting need addressing, but my suspicion is that we will only start making headway once the idea of Christian nurture is seen in terms of life-long learning. We have much to learn from the USA, where, free from the distraction of state RE provision in schools, there is a recognition of the responsibility of each faith community to provide education for those who belong to their tradition. We all should be going to Sunday School – even if it might be on a Monday! This observation stems from a conviction that there should be such a climate of learning in the church that the Church becomes "a Christian community where people discuss issues, raise questions, and learn more about themselves, their world, and their faith."[54] Ongoing nurture in the faith is so obviously important in other faith-traditions that one wonders why we seem to be floundering with it. One possible reason for our current educational malaise is that many of us have had bad experiences of Christian education ourselves. We are very reluctant, consequently, to treat it with due seriousness because our negative experiences of Sunday-school have become an inhibitor. Or, perhaps, we are so overcome by an apathetic and negative culture that we give up before we start? We may think that *they* do not want teaching. While, some of my experiences suggest that such thoughts and attitudes are understandable, there is real evidence to the contrary, eg the success of Alpha courses, the wide range of people studying Christianity related subjects in higher education establishments, and, even, the success of the 'Training for Learning and Service' course. People actually may be ready to respond to an educational emphasis in the church. My suspicion that this is so was kindled by hearing an Anglican vicar speak on local radio. He had been brought into the studio during a religious affair's programme to talk about the reasons why his congregation was growing. The Bishop had sent him to a rather run-down parish and given him carte-blanche to do what was necessary to turn things round. "If you fail, don't worry; give it one final go", seemed to have been the instruction. "So what did you do?" the interviewer asked. "Three things", said the vicar, "I sacked the organist, removed a third of the pews and increased the sermon to half an hour! We attended to our music. Now we have a new organist and a music group who are able to provide music of quality and variety in worship. Minus the rows of pews at the back of the church there is space to meet and talk. Before we got rid of them the congregation left, often only having spoken with me. Fellowship is crucial to church growth". "But what about lengthening the sermon?" enquired a rather incredulous interviewer? "In a sound-byte culture, I thought that was the very last thing to do!" "No!" said the vicar, "People are open to serious exploration of the Bible. It is crucial that people understand their faith, and we underestimate people's yearning for knowledge". Music in worship, fellowship and teaching: were the key elements in renewing the life of this particular congregation. Time and again, quality teaching (not always through preaching) is one of the features of a healthy church.

(iii) The Church as the School-house of Faith

One way of drawing out what I am advocating is to think of the church as 'the school-house of Faith'. The phrase echoes not only in our recent non-conformist past, but it also reminds us of the centrality of education in early examples of Dissent. The church is a learning environment in three senses. First, the Christian

---

[54]   Ibid. p 26.

community is a body to which people come in order to hear about things they do not already know. It shares a story with people which helps them to put a proper perspective on their lives. This primary purpose of the church, however, is not the one still most in evidence in our churches. Our churches are institutional providers of a range of activities, many of which have nothing particularly Christian about them, when our major purpose ought to concern putting people in touch with the Christian understanding of the meaning, purpose and destiny of life. Secondly, the church should be a place where a person's ongoing growth and struggle on the pilgrimage of life is encouraged. A highly confident style of church in which 'we' stand in judgement over the adequacy of 'their' faith still is all too common. The really healthy church is one in which a person's questions are taken seriously and sensitively explored, not one in which people are given ready-made slick answers. Thirdly, the church needs to be a body which centres on a solid base of teaching that is mutually owned. Part of the church's educational function is to be exploring that solid base in such a way that it is re-appropriated in new ways and owned again in each generation as if it were new. We have to develop ways of helping churches to find the ability to share that central core of teaching. The Alpha Course has provided one model from which we have a great deal to learn about getting into a position to talk about faith with those outside the church. Some, however, would wish for a methodology less bound to the middle-class dinner set and a rather more open-minded theological content – if never so open at both ends that what was once in the middle has merely run out!

Thomas R Hawkins' in *The Learning Congregation* recognises that a rapidly changing society – 'a permanent white-water society' (Vaill)[55] – needs organisations that are fast and flexible, participatory rather than hierarchical. Given the nature of churches we should immediately be aware of the kind of revolution he has in mind. Organisations in today's world need to be environments in which individuals are committed to growing, learning and creating. They are enabled to do so by being granted respect, given space to examine assumptions, encouragement to experiment and take risks, with failure being the necessary price to be paid on some occasions. In such organisations leaders educate by attending to the whole person and proceeding at the pace of the learner. When applied to churches, Hawkins challengingly talks about education as part of a person's sanctification, their growth towards the likeness of God. He also views Christian education holistically: it takes place in the home and community, not just inside the church. The church through learning remains the same while forever changing. What we pass on to others is partly ourselves changed through

---

[55]   Ibid. p 3.

the learning process. We thus all become teachers of the faith. However, "some individuals will always have a special responsibility for equipping people for continuous learning", argues Hawkins, in order to get over the practical problem of "something which is everyone's responsibility" running "the risk of becoming no one's responsibility."[56]

What, then, of ministry in 'the school-house of faith'? I have written in other places about the church's ongoing need for a well-prepared representative designated ministry: elders, ministers of word and sacrament and church-related community workers.[57] In short, ministers are needed to prepare the whole people of God for ministry, where 'ministry' is viewed more in the terms of a person's Christian vocation in society than them simply performing church functions. Not everyone is called to such a representative role, but we must remember that ministers are not called to do the church's work as much as put the church to work. Part of that task is educational: "The learning congregation, built around a renewed ministry of teaching and learning, equips the laity for their proper role as those who bear public witness to the gospel in their daily lives and work."[58] I care deeply about that ministry of teaching and learning. It is part of what today's church needs, although, I regret to say, often it does not seem to want it!

E. MISSIONARY CHURCH

'They devoted themselves to the apostle's teaching and fellowship, to the breaking of bread and the prayers'. But why did they do this? We can presume that one reason concerns the way in which such activities bring personal fulfilment to people. To be sure the church has a saddening ability to make them mind-numbingly dull and boring – but they needn't be. These central core activities of the 'encountering church' help us develop as persons, focus our lives in positive ways and are exciting to engage in. To put it in a nutshell, they are the means by which we encounter one another in Christ.

1. The Church as a Sacrament of God's Love

Before we take this legitimate line of thinking too far we need to be reminded that ultimately the church is not here to serve our purposes. Its life is to be shaped in response to the twin commandment of Jesus: the call to love God

---

[56]   Ibid. p 47.
[57]   See David R Peel, *Ministry for Mission* (Manchester: Northern College, 2003).
[58]   Hawkins, *The Learning Congregation*, p 66.

and our neighbour as ourselves. The church therefore lives for God and those beyond its fellowship. It is a means to an end: the giving of praise and glory to God and sacrificial service to others. As the teaching and example of Jesus amply demonstrates, there is an important sense whereby our sacrificial service to others becomes the means by which we most adequately offer praise and glory to God. A prophetic rather than priestly view of religion underpins the Jesus tradition. The parable of the Great Assize in which Jesus indicates that the ultimate judgement turns on our actions towards "the least of these who are members of my family" stands in a prophetic tradition which ridicules all religion that so attends to itself that it ignores the basic social and political injustices taking place in the society in which it is set. We find a classic example of this prophetic tradition in the witness of Isaiah of Jerusalem from the eighth century BCE:

> When you come to appear before me,
>   who asked this from your hand?
> Trample my courts no more;
>   bringing offerings is futile;
>   incense is an abomination to me.
> New moon and sabbath and calling of convocation –
>   I cannot endure solemn assemblies with iniquity.
> Your new moons and your appointed festivals my soul hates;
>   they have become a burden to me,
> I am weary of bearing them.
> When you stretch out your hands,
>   I will hide my eyes from you;
>   even though you make many prayers, I will not listen;
>   your hands are full of blood.
> Wash yourselves; make yourselves clean;
>   remove the evil of your doings from before my eyes;
>   cease to do evil,
>   learn to do good;
>   seek justice, rescue the oppressed,
>   defend the orphan, plead for the widow.
>
>   (Isaiah 1: 12-17)

And it was within this same prophetic tradition that Jesus stood when he made his programmatic statement at Nazareth:

The Spirit of the Lord is upon me,
  because he has anointed me
  to bring good news to the poor.
He has sent me to proclaim release to the captives
  and recovery of sight to the blind,
  to let the oppressed free,
  to proclaim the year of the Lord's favour.

(Luke 4: 18-19; Isaiah 61: 1-2)

"Today this scripture has been fulfilled in your hearing". Jesus was announcing the Jubilee when there was to be a radical re-distribution of wealth and fortune. And that presumably was why he got into trouble. ". . . all in the synagogue were filled with rage" (Luke 4: 28). Religion has a record of seeking to attend to God and forgetting our neighbour. Significantly, several theologians in the middle of the twentieth century called for a 'religionless Christianity', a phrase of Dietrich Bonhoeffer's which reflects Karl Barth's great tirade against 'religion'. Christian 'religion' had failed the real test when the Third Reich moved towards power, and, along with the biblical prophetic tradition before him, Barth pointed out how that religion was an abomination to God.

The church is a sign, an expression and an anticipation of God's kingdom, but this side of Eternity it never is the kingdom. The 'covenanting gathered body of saints' called 'church' is a sacrament in the sense that it is called to *re-present* to others the gift and obligation of God's love for all created things and persons. That gift and obligation is focussed for us in Jesus, the primal sacrament of God's love, and, consequently, the church's representative calling is to present before others that self-same gift and obligation of love. The church is a sacrament through which people receive God's gift of love, and from which people are sent to live and serve according to the rule of love. It is a community through which men and women encounter God as love and from which they are sent out to join in God's work of love amidst the world. The church is not the sole place of that encounter; rather, it is the community which announces that such encounters take place at the heart of ordinary life and it encourages people to seek them. God is alive and at work in our world. Set free from what the Bible calls sin, we are invited to join God in the divine liberating work. The church's task, therefore, is not only to draw people's attention to the grace being offered us once again by God in the cross of Jesus Christ; it also involves encouraging people to engage with God's work and preparing them to undertake it. Therein lays the church's mission.

2.   Problems with 'Mission'

In his magisterial book, *Transforming Mission: Paradigm Shifts in Theology of Mission*, David J Bosch reminds us that "Christianity is missionary by its very nature, or it denies its very *raison d'être*."[59] It points people towards an engagement with the *missio Dei*, God's mission of love in the world. When true to itself it will place before the world a *theology* which addresses the human predicament, an *ethic* which reflects our duty to love God and our neighbour as ourself and a *vision* which provides people with something to hope for that is worth them working towards. The mission of the church flows naturally from its counter-cultural shape. It involves costly encounter with the God who is already at work in the world.

But the word 'mission' is problematic. First of all, it cannot easily be liberated from its history. Or, to put it another way, 'mission' cannot be separated from 'missions' which, in the light of history, have not found the church behaving at her best. The problem, of course, is compounded for us by knowing that the crusading, imperialistic dimension of Christian outreach is still being replicated by some parts of the church today. Just as there was once a very dubious connection between the colonial aspirations of nations and the evangelistic activity of their churches (e.g. the British, Spanish and Portuguese during the period of missionary expansion in the eighteenth and nineteenth centuries) so today the activities of the religious 'Right' in the USA seem to underpin the American-driven 'globalization' project. Manipulation, bribery and, even, violence is part of this history. Those who have read their missionary histories can be forgiven for having problems with the word 'mission'. Mission comes to us with, as they say, 'previous'!

Secondly, and connected with this, is a fear that 'mission' when used in the church suffers from quite misplaced intentions. Indeed, quite often the church's perception of its mission undermines what its mission should really be. As we have seen, mission involves a theology, ethic and a vision which is rooted in selfless love: putting God and neighbour before self. But so often 'mission' is perceived in the quite selfish institutional terms of increasing the size of the church. The narrative which has informed this discussion about the 'Encountering Church' is very interesting at this point. It ends by saying: 'And day by day the Lord added to their number those who were being saved' (Acts 2: 47). The work of the church: fellowship, worship and teaching was the enabler of mission: proclamation and

---

[59]   David J. Bosch, *Transforming Mission: Paradigm Shifts in Theology of Mission* (Maryknoll, New York: Orbis Books, 1991), p 9.

service, that in turn led to church growth. Note the order: it wasn't 'how can *we* increase our numbers' leading to 'let's try to do a bit of mission' and on to a focus on 'fellowship, worship and teaching'. It was the reverse. As clearly as night follows day, attention to fellowship, worship and teaching leads to mission and, *if the Lord wills it*, then to church growth. Given the biblical logic of mission, we should always be prepared to contemplate the possibility that God does not want to add to our number, since what we are about has had its day, and however much we want to get others engaged in it God might actually have moved on!

Thirdly, it follows that mission is simply what a healthy church does naturally. Only sick and ailing churches discuss mission. When they do talk about it, they need to be directed to the more basic issues: fellowship, worship and teaching. We are being Spirit-driven into becoming encountering churches in response to the way in which we have truly encountered the God whom we have met in Jesus through our fellowship, worship and teaching. Attend to fellowship, worship and teaching and the missionary shape of being church naturally emerges. The church doesn't 'do' mission, it becomes mission as it aligns itself with the passion and purposes of God. Nor does the church construct mission statements out of its own head; it is given a task to be undertaken in obedience. And very often, the church has been most faithful when it has been institutionally troubled and numerically weak.

3. Defining 'Mission'

One of my colleagues goes into a highly critical mode whenever she hears people using the word 'mission'. 'Mission' like 'fellowship' is a weasel word, so devoid of precise meaning that we can all use it to mean different things, thereby papering over the cracks of many a vexed argument. It gets so 'watered down' that we can use it to refer to just about any church activity, or, when used in precise ways by determined people, it can be a means of claiming that a person's partial understanding of what mission entails is actually all that mission involves. Hence we see the word not only so diluted that it becomes meaningless, but also used to underpin forms of Christian exclusivity. It is important, therefore, to investigate the term further.

I suggest that *mission represents all the activity which takes place as Christians, living and working at the interface between church and society, engage in God's liberating work in the world.* In order to explain this more fully, I wish to draw attention to certain key things.

a) This understanding of mission presupposes that the Christian church has a God-shaped identity which makes it distinct if never fully separate from society. Here we renew our acquaintance with the idea that the church is 'in the world, but not of the world'. Mission then in some sense is a counter-cultural activity. When listening to the church, society needs to hear more than its own music.

b) This understanding of mission recognises that mission belongs to God and that our task is to follow an invitation to engage with what God is already doing. It is not about us scratching our heads to invent a programme. That is to put the cart before the horse. The fact that this is what we usually do doesn't make it right!

c) Mission takes place 'at the interface between church and society'. It is not church based, nor can it be fully reduced to humanistic activity in the secular world. It is the stuff of an encounter between a community seeking to be God-shaped and a society that God is in the process of shaping. This encounter is not that simply or necessarily between the 'Godly' and the 'Godless' since God is at work on both sides of the encounter. What is true, loving and just is found in God, but it is never fully manifested by either side. The church no less than society is on a journey of discovery. As the church receives from a society within which God is always at work, its story is always in the process of being given new life in the telling of it. Required texts for all who wish to understand the dynamic of missionary encounter are those which deal with Jesus' meeting with the Canaanite woman (Matthew 15: 21-28) and Peter's meeting with Cornelius (Acts 10). Both indicate the phenomenon of the 'evangelisation of the evangeliser'. Christian mission will just as likely change the church as society.

d) Mission is an act of obedience. Its invitation to people is not so much a request to 'come to us' as an invitation to 'join us in following him'. At its heart is God's generous invitation to engage in God's mission. The *missio Dei*, therefore, is a collaborative project, and because of God's threefold nature, the mission we are invited to join is a multi-faceted activity. A common, collective purpose is given by the unity of God being God; a diverse expression and experience of the divine work is signalled by God's trinitarian diversity. It is totally unlikely and actually utterly impossible that any of us will be involved in every aspect involved in mission. Indeed, it is sufficient to know that, due to the gifts and aptitudes we have been given, we each have our own particular roles to play. Mission is a 'one size fits all' kind of phenomenon. There is something with which everyone can engage in God's mission; none of us is called to do everything.

4.   A Redundant Debate

We are now in a position to hear some more missiological wisdom from David Bosch:

> Mission is a multifaceted ministry, in respect of witness, service, justice, healing, reconciliation, liberation, peace, evangelism, fellowship, church planting, contextualization, and much more. And yet, even the attempt to list some dimensions of mission is fraught with danger, because it again suggests that we can define what is infinite. Whoever we are, we are tempted to incarcerate the *missio Dei* in the narrow confines of our own predilections, thereby of necessity reverting to one-sidedness and reductionism. We should beware of any attempt at delineating mission too sharply.[60]

Once the vastness and diversity of God is appreciated, we start to appreciate the impossibility of ever being able to engage fully in everything involved in God's mission enterprise. Nor, as Bosch reminds us, can we 'define what is infinite'. Mission, nevertheless, has often become a battle-ground in the church partly because various sides have entered the debate with rather narrow understandings about mission. Throughout my ministry, I have been troubled by the quarrel between so-called 'evangelicals' who have stressed what we might caricature as the 'soul saving' dimension of mission and the so-called 'liberals' who have stressed the 'society changing' dimension. According to their caricatures, the evangelical is always in danger of robbing mission of its social and political thrust, while the liberal tends to ignore the depth of God's liberating work; the evangelical invites people to 'identify' with the saving faith proclaimed by the church, the liberal encourages people to seek the peace and justice of the world. When taken to the extreme, the evangelical tendency is sectarianism, with the inevitable danger of simply failing to 'connect' with our culture, while the liberal faces the opposite problem of becoming so wrapped up in worldly affairs that it has nothing to say to the world. I repeat: this is a caricature – but we can all recognise the quarrel, perhaps even having participated in it!

If the understanding of mission I'm advocating is accepted both sides in this dispute are vindicated: Yes, mission does involve challenging people with the judgement and grace of God which calls people to re-orientate their lives,

---

[60]   Ibid. p 512.

---

away from self and towards God and neighbour; and, yes, mission does involve wholehearted commitment to engage with the God of freedom and justice in changing the face of this earth. But both sides are also in danger of 'heresy', that way of looking at things which is not simply the advocacy of out and out falsehood but much more a case of believing that part of the truth is in fact the whole truth. It seems clear, to echo Kant, that the Word without the deed is dumb, and the deed without the Word is empty. It is also clear, that the world always needs to hear what evangelicals and liberals have championed in their distinctive ways. And, thankfully, I think many of us now can see this. It is, of course, one of the important features of post-modern culture that people are able to 'pick and mix'. This is often looked down on disparagingly, and so it should be if it means people just picking the bits they fancy or the things that make them feel good. But it can also testify to the ability of recognising the 'hybridity' of truth and the way in which a mature approach to living involves many layers of insight. 'Both and' may be typical of British compromises, but such a strategy is absolutely central to an incarnational faith which is rooted in 'heaven' *and* 'earth', and in an inclusive church which is united yet diverse.

A most recent ecumenical consensus on 'mission' produced the so-called 'Five Marks of Mission':

- to proclaim the good news of the kingdom
- to teach, baptise and nurture new believers
- to respond to human need by loving service
- to seek to transform unjust structures of society
- to strive to safeguard the integrity of creation, to sustain and renew the life of earth

We can note the degree of diversity which betrays a noble intention to be inclusive. Elsewhere, I have described elsewhere the 'Five Marks' as 'imaginative and helpful'.[61] Conservative evangelicals who tend to stress the first two are reminded of the last three, which so often are championed by liberals, and, of course, visa versa. It is easy to suggest ways in which this definition is inadequate. That is the way it always will be with attempts to describe mission. Notwithstanding the fact that few churches have actually considered their life and witness in relation to the 'Five Marks', this particular piece of missiological thinking has a great deal to comment it.

---

[61]   See Peel, *Ministry for Mission*, p 53.

5.   Two Key Questions and a Hunch

By way of conclusion, I would like to leave you three conclusions about mission. Two come in the shape of questions; the other is more of a hunch. All three are exciting, if very challenging.

(i)   Central to my conviction about God's universality is a belief that, while the activity of God in the world may be *defined* by the Christ-event, it is not *confined* to the narrow stream of witness to God which flows from it. God was at work before Jesus, and God is at work outside the church. How then does the mission of the church relate to the existence of non-Christian faiths and ideologies? To make the point by quoting the title of a book: *Is There Only One True Religion Or Are There Many?*[62] This is a crucial question for all to address in our multi-faith society. Some Christians answer negatively[63]; others answer positively;[64] most plot a path somewhere between the two.[65] In a recent book, someone who tends towards a positive answer to the question as to whether or not there is more than one true religion has suggested that people view the matter in four ways.[66] *Replacement*: Christianity, the sole true religion replaces all other faiths; *fulfilment*: Christianity is the fulfilment of all religions; *mutuality*: all the great world faiths are mutually valid ways to the Truth; *acceptance*: we work for convergence between religions but recognise irreconcilable features of other faiths in relation to Christianity. My approach is to say that while *in principle* there may be more than one true religion, *in practice* only God knows! Meanwhile, we can only testify to what we have 'seen' through the Christian tradition in conversation with those whose faith-experience differs to our own.

---

[62]   Schubert M. Ogden, *Is There Only One True Religion or Are There Many?* (Dallas, Texas: Southern Methodist University Press, 1992).
[63]   Note the classical 'Outside The Church, No Salvation' claims of pre-Vatican II Catholicism and, on the Protestant side, the work of Hendrik Kraemer in *The Christian Message in a Non-Christian World* (New York: Harper Row and London: Edinburgh House Press, 1938 and, of course, Karl Barth, *Church Dogmatics*, 1/2 (Edinburgh: T & T Clark, 1956). Less sophisticated expressions of 'exclusivism' are common place among the members of the Christian Right.
[64]   The most well-known example is John Hick. See his *God and the Universe of Faiths* (London and Basingstoke: The Macmillan Press Ltd, 1973) and *An Interpretation of Religion: Human Responses to the Transcendent* (New Haven, Conn.: Yale University Press, 1989).
[65]   See the work of the revisionary Roman Catholic theologian Karl Rahner in his *Theological Investigations* (London: Darton, Longman and Todd), 5 (1966), 6 (1969), 14 (1976) and 16 (1979). Also see Gavin D'Costa, *Theology and Religious Pluralism: The Challenge of Other Religions* (Oxford: Basil Blackwell, 1986).
[66]   See Paul F. Knitter, *Introducing Theologies of Religions* (Maryknoll, NY: Orbis Books, 2002).

(ii)   At several points I have stressed that God's work is not confined to the church. God is at work in the world, and the task of the church is to help people discover precisely that fact. One way of understanding Christian history is to view it in terms of the church perpetually re-inventing itself to respond to what it believed God to be requiring of it. In many different places Christianity bedded into the local culture by telling the Christian story in ways that addressed the living issues of the locality. So, to use an early example, the New Testament reveals the tense process whereby Christianity became the faith of the Gentile as well as Jew. The church has always been multi-cultural. We are now living in a post-Christendom culture, a culture quite different to the one in which most of our churches were founded. How will the church now respond to its context? Some will think in terms of Church expansion, extending what we have inherited into the new culture, making the odd adjustment here and there, but largely inviting a post-Christendom world to return to the supposed halcyon days of yesteryear. Others will argue for drastic measures as they see the traditional patterns of churchgoing breaking down and the institutional churches cutting little ice in the modern world. What is required, they will argue, are new ways of being church that start where people are and hence become new patterns of Christianity which are woven out of the fabric of contemporary culture. The church has always felt the need to reform itself in order to be a faithful vehicle for God's reformation of persons and peoples. Missionary needs have always shaped the church. What kind of shape do we now need to be in if we are to be faithful? Are we required and, if so, are we willing to die that we may be reborn in our contemporary culture? Whichever way we answer this question we must never forget that there never was, nor ever will be, one way of being church.

(iii)   I have stressed the fact that, in David Bosch's words, "It is not the church which is 'undertaking' mission; it is the *missio Dei* which constitutes the church."[67] Mission is akin to an attribute of God, and as such it not only precedes the church but actually brings it into being. With the *missio Dei* there wouldn't have been the church. It follows that the church will only ever possess a proper sense of purpose when it is aligned to God's mission. And, hence, my hunch is that what we need today is not ever more 'activism' but the discovery of that kind of spiritual depth which only comes from giving attention to God, waiting on God and learning what God would have us be and do. The crisis in the church is not about structures or resources; it is about locating the Spirit. The great vision we need to catch is essentially spiritual.

---

67   Bosch, *Transforming Mission*, p 519.

CHAPTER FIVE

IN THE WORLD BUT NOT OF THE WORLD:
The Challenge of being a Counter-cultural Church

It was a great privilege to have been invited to deliver the St Columba's lecture, not simply because of the honour which comes with such invitations, but also because preparing for the lecture helped me to work out more thoroughly the theme I had chosen for my year as Moderator of General Assembly: *Encountering Church*.[68] As I have been moving around the United Reformed Church I have been reminding people of the way in which congregations are called to be places of real encounter, where through learning, fellowship and worship we engage with one another in ways that enable us to meet God anew in a vitally fresh manner. This line of thinking has involved my arguing that when congregations focus on their core activities they discover their mission. It is through attending to learning, fellowship and worship that we find out what God is doing in the world and become equipped to play our part in God's mission.[69] Very often, however, we get so caught up with the need to keep the institution going that we are in danger of loosing sight of what the church is called to be, namely, the sacrament of God's love in the world, the community whose words and deeds are to play a part in God's mission. At the same time that the United Reformed Church through its 'Catch the Vision' programme recently has focussed its attention upon our un-wieldy structures, it has been an appropriate counterpoint for its Assembly Moderator to be reminding folk about some of the things our structures are meant to support and service in obedience and loyalty to God.

In this lecture I want to move beyond the encounters in learning, fellowship and worship which are the life-blood of congregational life. What seems crucial for the churches' future is that we develop a theological awareness of what we are about in our relation to the world beyond the church. This will partly be a response to what we believe God to be asking of us, but it also will need to

---

68   This lecture began as a sermon preached at the North East Oecumenical Course's Summer School at Luther King House, Manchester on the 7th August 2005. Under the influence of ideas which 'came' to me during the CTE Church Leaders' Consultation, 13th and 14th September 2005, and via an address to the Southern Synod of the United Reformed Church on 8th October 2005, the lecture found its present shape. It was delivered on the 31st October 2005.

69   This thinking is based on a consideration of the Jerusalem church we read about in Luke-Acts (see Acts 2:42-47, 4: 32-35, 5: 12-16). What I call the 'core activities' of learning, fellowship and worship are taken from Acts 2: 42.

---

involve finding an ecclesial shape which meets the challenges and the needs of the age – not least because the shape we are in at present in many places is clearly inappropriate. If we were given the luxury today of starting out afresh as churches only in a relative few cases would we choose to replicate the Christian institutions we have in our cities, towns and villages. But this observation is merely the tip of the ice-berg when it comes to the negative critique of the contemporary church to which we must now respond. Some would say that the major reason why we need to re-discover what should be involved at the church-society interface is found in the simple fact that what we have inherited is clearly failing. Lest we become over simplistic, though, it is advisable that we consider in more detail what I've just described as 'the negative critique of the contemporary church.' It comes in at least three forms: the secularist, the statistical and the theological.

The Negative Critique of the Contemporary Church

The first form of the negative critique of the contemporary church is launched from outside the church, often by intellectuals and particularly those who regard all religions as trading in superstition. This secularist challenge is to the church *per se*, not just to the church in its present manifestation. An enlightened age like ours, the rationalist argument runs, has out-grown what the churches stand for: reason has replaced revelation as the basis of our understanding; God is merely a projection of human wish fulfilment. It is further claimed that given its track-record for generating conflict, religion needs exposing for being what one advocate of this critique calls "the most ferociously divisive force"[70] in the contemporary world. Many contemporary politicians dismiss their opponents' positions as mere 'theology', thereby equating the thought-system which underpins religion with utter sophistry. Those who are committed to the community called church are looked on condescendingly as people who have yet to become fully adult in our secular age. To be sure, it riles *The Guardian* columnist Polly Toynbee that a recent debate in the House of Lord's on a bill concerned with assisted dying for the terminally ill was "a reminder of how strongly the religions still flavour our national discussion, how much they influence government thinking".[71] It also baffles the 1960's prophets of atheism that people still confess to having belief in a transcendent being in roughly the same numbers as they did forty years ago. And, as we shall see, during the last twenty years there has been increasing awareness and pursuit of the spiritual dimension in life. Indeed, so strong has been the popular movement away from

---

[70]   Polly Toynbee. 'The bishops have no right to restrict our right to die' in *The Guardian*, 14 October 2005.

[71]   Ibid. The influence of the churches on government thinking was also in evidence in the concessions gained by ecumenically lobbying on the 2005 Gambling Bill.

---

supporting the secularization hypothesis that Clive Marsh, the Methodist theologian, has called our post-modern era the "post-atheist" age.[72] Those who believe theistic belief is inherently childish, and something which one-day human beings will grow out of, must find it either bemusing or galling that equally intelligent people are on hand to challenge their rationalistic outlook as vigorously as they advance it.[73] Indeed, it has even been argued that the arrogance and lack of charity displayed by some contemporary atheists helps the cause of religion. Dylan Evans, for example, suggests that Richard Dawkins' "attacks on religion are so vitriolic and bad-tempered that they alienate the sensitive reader and give atheism a bad name."[74]

Whatever the truth of Evans' suggestion, it needs noting that this secularist challenge to the church is as markedly modern as it is western. Michael Paul Gallagher of the Gregorian University in Rome challenges us "to question the credentials of unbelief as normal and neutral", and he observes that

> A "faithless" culture is unnatural and exceptional from the point of view of world history or of today's world geography. We happen to live in a section of the world where non-religion seems dominant, but seen globally that is a minority view.[75]

Since minorities are sometimes right, though, the church cannot take it for granted that the secularist challenge will self-destruct. It has been recognised for a long time that there sometimes falls upon Christians the responsibility to defend publicly what we believe (see 1 Peter 3: 15). This involves not only showing how what we say and do as Christians is authorised by the witness of Jesus in life and through death, but it also entails demonstrating the credibility of our witness in today's world. This will not be easy to achieve in our anti-intellectual ecclesial culture, where commitment to being a learning church is way down the church meeting agenda, and people are fearful of talking about their faith, even among themselves. But it is central to the challenge of being Christian today.

The second form of the negative critique of the contemporary church is statistical. Membership figures of the churches are collected over a period of time, trends are observed and predictions are made about the future. And, as

---

72   Note the title of Clive Marsh's, *Christianity in a Post-Atheist Age* (London: SCM Press, 2002).
73   The recent public debates between Richard Dawkins and Keith Ward clearly show that as rational a case can be made out for theism as is advanced for atheism. It is not self-evident that "the few worshippers in the *real* world" (Polly Toynbee, n2 above-italics mine) are atheists.
74   Dylan Evans, 'The 21st Century Atheist', *The Guardian*, 2 May 2005.
75   Michael Paul Gallagher, 'Struggle and Conversion', *The Tablet*, 10 September 2005.

we all know, the predictions are invariably bleak, with the only contested point being when the church will die due to lack of numbers. This critique views organisational health in numerical terms. Largely a product of the computer era, it is the scene of some rank bad science. It is very misleading to examine past and present church attendance statistics and then use them as the solid basis for futurology. Factors unknown to us now are just as likely to alter tends in the future as the downward spiral of church attendance is of continuing. To use a trivial example to make a basic point: in April 2005 we might have predicted that, based on the trend over say the past fifteen years, there would be less people interested in cricket in England a year later in April 2006. That prediction is almost certain to be wrong because an unexpected event took place which altered things, namely the Ashes victory. It is as difficult to predict that the one in four URC churches that are numerically growing will continue to grow as it is to predict that the three in four that are numerically declining will continue to decline. Cinema going is now increasingly popular after decades of decline and those who focus positively on the pockets of vibrant Christianity that are around will tell us that something similar may well be happening with church attendance. It may, or it may not, we cannot know for sure.

The cynic in each one of us will recall that "There are three kinds of lies – lies, damned lies and statistics" (Mark Twain). However, the experience of most of us actually does confirm some of the negativity of this statistical challenge. When I reflect upon what has happened to many of the churches I know in the North of England I cannot deny that they have been declining, nor can I do anything other than be concerned about whether they have a future. We have been witnessing an era in which large numbers of people have been contracting out of institutional religion. This has left huge question marks over the future of many churches, but it also poses the challenge to us of being church in relevant and faithful ways so that the un-churched members of our very religious age contract into the movement which maintains the precious and subversive memory of Jesus and keeps that memory alive in its encounters with society.

Both the secularist and statistical critiques of the church carry force since, however flawed we may deem them to be, they point to the church's need to present a faith and practice that will stand up, be recognised and be responded to by people who at present pass us by. But a far greater challenge to us comes from an internal theological critique that can always be made of the church. Consider the following statements:

We look at our half empty churches today, almost negligible from the politicians' point of view, treated by some parties with hollow patronage, by other parties with malicious insolence; the butt of third-rate novelists and the shortest way to a cheap sneer. We look at the unexampled devotion in the village and the suburb and the city of the few who in fact maintain these churches; we remind ourselves how few are the motives except simple piety that can draw men [*sic* and women] to serve the church today; we consider the world-wide missionary activity ceaselessly maintained by this handful of Church people in an indifferent nation.[76]

The condition of our churches . . . in great cities, in country towns and in villages, is itself often almost desperate . . . Our dreadful weakness is religious. We are not declaring the Gospel with power to a dispirited and disillusioned age; we are not living in the discipline of Gospel fellowship; only in a very imperfect degree are our churches God's resting place and holy habitation.[77]

. . . a missionary focus ought to be central to our understanding of the church. This involves rediscovering a gospel faithfulness to re-present God's Word of selfless love to those outside the church. It also suggests that we must be prepared for an ecclesial revolution as we grasp the demands of the hour and effect a change of ethos: from our churches being inward-looking and largely self-serving organisations to their becoming part of a movement whose very purpose is to reform individuals and reshape society; from temple buildings to tent living; and from Christian gathering to escape from the world to their meeting to engage with the society in which they are called to be a sacrament of God's love.[78]

There is power and passion in those statements. They span over seventy-five years, but each describes our contemporary church scene very well. The first comes from Bernard Lord Manning, addressing the Assembly of the Congregational Union of England and Wales in 1927. Manning, of course, was a Cambridge man so, given where I'm speaking, there had to be an Oxford counter-point. Hence the second statement comes from the pen of Nathaniel Micklem. He is reflecting on the Congregational scene of the 1950's, the era of Macmillan's 'You've never had it so good' – when I was only a lad in the Sunday-school of a very strong and active Congregational church. The 'religious' weakness to which Micklem points was largely responsible, I believe, for the rapid decline of that church, along with

---

76   Bernard Lord Manning, *Essays in Orthodox Dissent* (London: Independent Press Ltd., 1939).
77   Nathaniel Micklem, *The Box and the Puppets* (London: Geoffrey Bles, 1957). p 94.
78   David R. Peel, *Mission for Ministry* (Manchester: Northern College, 2003). p 31.

many others in the North of England. The former Principal of Mansfield College knew full well that, in the words of, P T Forsyth, "A bustling institution may cover spiritual destitution, just as Christian work may be taken up as a narcotic to spiritual doubt and emptiness."[79] The third statement was written by me a couple of years ago, a touch of red-brick amidst the Oxbridge glitter!

The three statements reveal two matters of huge significance to us as we move towards a theological awareness of what we need to be about as churches in our relation to a largely un-churched world. First, we are reminded that the state of the church of our childhood was not as rosy as we are sometimes prone to think. A lot of things I hear being said about some past halcyon church era are more nostalgia than reality, the product of rose-tinted spectacled observation. Not only are things not as hopeless with the contemporary church as the secularist and statistical critiques argue, but also things were not as well with our churches in the past as some people's memories would seem to suggest.

Secondly and more importantly, the statements clearly show that any observant critic can point to awful weaknesses in any church at any time, however numerically weak or strong they happen to be. Churches reflect the human natures of their members. Wheat as well as tares grow until the harvest. There is always a gap between what we are called to be and do and what in reality we are and actually do. Arguably, it is easier to find the gap in our larger churches, since there's no place for the half-hearted or uncommitted church member to hide in a smaller community of the gathered saints. The churches of the 1920s were numerically strong when compared with many churches in the contemporary United Reformed Church, but in Manning's view what made a church strong was not their numerical size but the 'simple piety' of their members. Equally numerically strong when compared to many of today's churches were those of the 1950s in which Micklem found a woeful weakness, not a lack of members so much as a 'religious' weakness, an inability to communicate and live out the gospel. Whether a church is numerically small or large, the proper test of its health is found in the 'simple piety' of its members, in whether it is deeply 'religious', in its faithfulness. That test is theological rather than statistical: Is the life of a particular church such a celebration of the gospel that people are caught up in the ongoing Triune life of God? Is the church in question through its shape and substance reforming individuals and changing society into more Christlike patterns and ways? Such questions provide us with the underlying theological reasons why it

---

[79]   P.T.Forsyth, *Positive Preaching and the Modern Mind* (London: Independent Press Ltd., 1907) p 117.

---

is important that we address the question of the churches relationship with what lies beyond it. To help us do this I propose to use Paul's letter to the Romans as a conversation partner.

The Roman Church

The first church in Rome was multi-cultural, as one might expect in a cosmopolitan city of the first century. In that church were not only Jews, members of the race to whom belonged the very first witnesses to Jesus as the Christ, but also so-called Gentiles, members of the wider non-Jewish cultural mix of the Empire's Capital. One of the many periods of political upheaval in Rome saw tremendous persecution of the Jewish community under Claudius in AD49.[80] This persecution of the Jews most likely had a knock-on effect in the Roman church: as the Jews were driven out of Rome the Roman church became less multi-cultural and more mono-cultural. And very quickly a pattern of being church would have developed which, quite understandably, now fitted a Gentile culture, no longer having to take into account Jewish cultural norms. Eventually, the authorities adopted a less hostile attitude to the Jews, with the result that Jewish people returned to Rome to pursue their trade and business interests, and the Christians among them most likely returned to the Roman church. You can imagine how they felt: once their church had been multi-cultural, respecting their Jewish culture; but now they were confined solely to eating vegetable at the meals held in their house-church, since all the meat on offer was non-kosher (Romans 14: 2).

Given this likely context, it is hardly surprising that one of the over-arching themes of the letter to the Romans is Christian inclusivity. Part of the burden of the epistle, consequently, is a challenge to its Roman readers to become or, perhaps, set about returning to being, a multi-cultural church: one in which Jew and Gentile followed Christ hand in hand, with the so-called 'weak' united with the so-called 'strong'.[81] Paul's missionary logic is quite clear: the gospel is not the possession of any single group; it is Good News for all. The story of God's love for the world, decisively re-presented in the life and teaching, death and resurrection of Jesus, is so universally important that it cannot be left residing in one particular cultural community. It was the kind of message that needed sharing with everyone, even if that meant the church going through upheavals to accommodate

---

[80]   At Acts 18: Iff we are introduced to Aquila and Priscilla, the famous and wealthy couple who had fled Rome in the wake of the A49 persecution. They meet Paul at Corinth, the likely place at which Romans was written.

[81]   For Paul's use of the terms 'weak' and 'strong' see Romans 14: 1 – 15: 6.

---

the needs of people who were different to the prevailing cultural make-up of the church, and even if that meant, as it most certainly did mean, a direct challenge to the Emperor. To proclaim 'Jesus is Lord' in the first century Rome was simply to court trouble; after-all the political authorities took it for granted that Caesar, not Jesus, was Lord.

The Post-modern West: Rome Re-visited?

A great deal has been made lately about the way in which Western culture during the twentieth century 'turned' from being 'Christian' to 'post-Christian'. This observation can be illustrated by reference to a number of factors: the growth of secularism (even if that growth has not been as extensive or thorough-going as the 1960's sociologists predicted); the presence among us of the so-called 'other faiths', reminding us daily of alternatives to the Christian narrative which also seek to address the deep issues surrounding the nature and destiny of human beings, societies and the cosmos; the questioning of all imposed authorities, which kindles the now wide-spread belief that the institutional churches have largely outlived both their relevance and usefulness. All these factors are more in evidence today than when I was being brought up in a Congregationalist family in the 1950s. During my life-time, two generations have grown up with hardly any more relationship to Christianity than had the majority of the citizens of the Roman Empire in the days of the Apostle Paul.

To be sure, some sociologists – Grace Davie in particular – have drawn attention to the fact that while the current members of our society show very little evidence of wanting to 'belong' to religious institutions like churches they, statistically at least, nevertheless confess that they broadly 'believe' in the things religions seek to represent.[82] And there also is evidence to suggest that people are more 'spiritually' conscious now than say twenty years ago. Indeed, the statistics are revealing. From research conducted over a fifteen year period we find between 1987 to 2002 a 90% rise in the numbers who see a purposeful patterning in events, a 41% rise in those who feel a divine presence in their lives, a 48% rise in those who believe prayers are answered, an 81% rise in those who sense the sacred in nature, a 39% increase in those who claim to experience the influence of the departed in their lives.[83] What passes for 'belief' among the 'believing' who do not 'belong' that I meet, however, is usually so far removed from anything

---

[82]   Grace Davie, *Religion in Britain since 1945: Believing Without Belonging* (Oxford UK & Cambridge USA: Blackwell 1994).

[83]   Statistics presented to the 'Where's Your Church In A Spiritual Age?' conference in Newcastle on the 28th January 2004.

---

resembling what I know as Christian believing that I tend to think that it would be for easier for us if we were facing folk who actually were outright unbelievers. Indeed, with many we face the greatest missiological challenge of all: addressing people who are totally apathetic about not only what we represent, but also the very fact we exist at all.

As we have already noted, futurology based upon computer predictions is somewhat unscientific. But not everything in the following list of claims is fanciful, if my own experiences with the un-churched are anything to go by: mainstream religions are being replaced by new spiritualities; paganism will be the largest religion in 25 years; New Age type 'worship' is now as common as mainstream Christian worship: religious language now is no longer understood beyond the communities who use it; Christianity has lost the high moral ground in our society.[84] At the very least, we ought to recognise that being British and being Christian are no longer synonymous. The world Paul was addressing when he wrote his letter to the Romans has far more in common with our world than I ever dreamt could be the case when I first studied Romans as an undergraduate. Like other New Testament writings which address similar contexts, Romans presents pertinent and prophetic challenges to our new missionary age. And, particularly, apposite is what I call 'Paul's missionary logic':

> For, 'Everyone who calls on the name of the Lord shall be saved'
> But how are they to call on one whom they have not believed?
> And how are they to believe in one whom they have never heard?
> And how are they to hear without someone to proclaim him? And
> how are they to proclaim him unless they are sent?
>
> (Romans 10: 13-15(a))

The issue then as well as now is not whether evangelism is required: that is self-evident. Rather, the issue concerns the appropriate ways in which the church engages with the prevailing culture. Should we be counter-cultural, insisting upon our inherited identity, and thus possibly giving in to that sectarian tendency which makes a virtue of the church's seemingly inherent inability to connect with the outside world? Or should we try to find new expressions of the gospel, and hence new ways of being church, ones that begin where people are, build upon their presuppositions and affirm their assumptions, thereby risking giving in to that reductionism tendency which cuts Christianity down to what the age finds acceptable? Jürgen Moltmann has called this "the identity-involvement dilemma".[85]

---

[84]   Ibid.
[85]   Jürgen Moltmann, *The Crucified God* (London: SCM Press, 1974) p 7.

Counter-Cultural Church

The church is a sign, expression and foretaste of God's kingdom, announced and inaugurated but not completed by Jesus. It is sacramental in the sense that through its life it is called to re-present Christ to those outside the community – the same Christ who is the primal sacrament of God's reign of love in the world. The church's sacramental function to re-present Jesus' work through witness, suffering and even death involves us placing before the world a distinctive pattern of thought-through living. This should include three elements: first a theology which addresses the human predicament in which we find ourselves. This theology will need to be adequate to our context as well as appropriate to the Christian witness of faith which is anchored in the early Church's witness to Jesus. Secondly, it ought to involve an ethic, which in both the private and public domains takes up God's invitation to love, not only love of the One who encounters us graciously ever anew in Jesus, but also our neighbours – not least those who Jesus described as ' the least of these who are members of my family' (Matthew 25: 40, 45). And thirdly it requires vision: providing people with something for which to hope. This has to be something that is worth working towards, and which we are prepared to defend in suffering and unto death, and inevitably this means that we cannot avoid becoming counter-cultural. As an Anglican friend said recently, claiming to quote Roman Williams, an element of sectarianism befits the true church.

The church is called to make a difference by being different. If we are to become an agent of transformation in our society and beyond we need to be offering ideas, behaviour and vision which may well be contrary to what is culturally normative. Faced with living in a world of grave inequality, hideous consumerism and rampant individualism the church is challenged to offer an alternative to what many people actually know deep down is getting us nowhere, is making us ill, is oppressive to the poor and is threatening the very existence of the planet, an alternative woven out of the interaction of the biblical witness to Jesus with all the possibilities and problems of our age. We may think it odd that Anglicans like Rowan Williams who live in the tradition of Establishment should be commending a counter-cultural church strategy, but before we arrogantly remind them that Establishment is part of the unfinished business of the Reformation let us in the Reformed tradition humbly recognize that our members, no less than our Anglican friends, tend to be wedded to a prevailing world view which cannot be squared with the Christian gospel as that is grounded in the early Christian witness to Jesus. When people look in the Christian mirror today they all too often merely see a reflection of the world which is the cause of their misery, pain and despair. It is difficult for us to accept that the gospel not only stands over against the world, but also over against the church, given that the church is part of the same sinful world and inevitably bound up with it. Accept the truth, though, we must: the church no less than our society stands under the judgment of the same gospel.

In a Christmas article in 2005, Madeline Bunting wrote of her hopes for the Roman Catholic Church. She observed that: "For all the considerable and, in many respects, desirable increases in personal freedom, the aggressively materialistic secular democracies of the west have not reduced the sum of human suffering nor increased the sum of happiness".[86] Then she went on to say that, the church – if I may be allowed to stretch her argument beyond Catholicism – has "a huge contribution to make to the understanding of the predicaments the human race faces: the global extremes of wealth and poverty, the environment, the tragedy of depression and loneliness".[87] It's the business of the church to set forth alternatives, not baptize the age in which we live as Christian. Those 'alternatives' must be allowed to set the agenda for a church which needs to be seen in future perhaps more as the people's movement it first was than the tired institution it has been allowed to become. With a hint of warning, Madeline Bunting then ended her article by saying that unless the Roman Catholic leadership "focus on today, within a few decades [the] pews, even at Christmas, will be looking very empty".[88] Responsible church leaders today will need to act partly as ecclesial undertakers helping us to lay to rest dead ways of being church, and thus enabling us to move on and discover new life. We will guard the heritage best though when our church leaders also act as ecclesial mid-wife's who help us bring new ways of being church into the world.

Culture-shaped Church

While it seems abundantly clear that we should emphasise today the counter-cultural dimension of being church, we should also recognise counter-culturalism's counterpoint. *The church also makes a difference to people by being the same as them.* In order to be understandable and relevant we have to meet people on their ground, to learn how to speak their language and to address their deepest needs and aspirations. What constitutes the Christian 'good news' has always been partly a function of the 'bad news' of the culture in which the church has variously found itself. The missiologists call this 'inculturalization' – providing the gospel with clothes suitable for a particular culture, and they speak

---

86   *The Guardian*, 20 December 2004.
87   Ibid.
88   Ibid.

of 'contextualization' – expressing the gospel in terms that address the dynamics of the age. To connect with people outside the church we must in significant ways become the same as them. Otherwise, we are engaging in what amounts to a dialogue of the deaf.

The Apostle Paul was not just counter-cultural; he was also a man of the people: 'I became all things to all people that I might save some' (1 Corinthians 9: 22). I guess that explains why some of the radical sections of the church get so exasperated with Paul. He was prepared to get involved with all the messy compromises which occur in genuine attempts at mission. But 'messy compromises' are inevitable in a people's movement that models itself upon the Incarnation: God becoming one of us so that we can be one with God. Wouldn't it have been much less messy if God had settled with being counter-cultural? Wouldn't it have been neater if God had not got the divine hands soiled with human? Perhaps, but God chose not to go down that route! Paul actually provides us with the most well-known account of God's ensuing model of mission:

> Let the same mind be in you that was in Christ Jesus,
>   who, though he was in the form of God,
>   did not regard equality with God
>   as something to be exploited,
>   but emptied himself,
>   taking the form of a slave,
>   being born in human likeness.
>   And being found in human form,
>   he humbled himself
>   and became obedient to the point of death –
>   even death on a cross.
>
> Therefore God also highly exalted him
>   and gave him the name
>   that is above every name,
>   so that at the name of Jesus
>   every knee should bend,
>   in heaven and on earth and under the earth,
>   and every tongue should confess
>   that Jesus Christ is Lord,
>   to the glory of God the Father.
>
>   (Philippians 2: 5-11)

The only model of mission which has credibility is one which the church fashions after the Incarnation. This spurns imperialistic pretensions and chooses the way of humility; it discovers real strength in genuine weakness; it finds victory the other side of defeat.

Many has been the wise missionary who has returned to their sending church with a confession: "While I thought I was taking Christ to the people, when I got there I found that Christ had long since arrived." Another way of putting this is to say that in the church's missionary engagement with a non-church culture, God is active on both sides of the encounter. As long as God is as we have found God to be in Jesus then we ought never to succumb to the temptation of viewing the world beyond the church as totally Godless. Of course, the church has often entered the missionary encounter assuming God was solely on its side of the engagement. We hear loud echoes of that self-same approach in certain contemporary strategies being advanced for Christian mission today in our post-Christendom culture. But there is more value and worth in the world beyond the church than many a Calvinist has supposed, simply because God has been at work there as well as with those who keep alive the precious memory of Jesus. One thing certainly required of Christians in our engagement with contemporary culture is affirmation of what we can, engagement with fellow 'people of goodwill', and learning about what is really going on 'out there'. When Peter, the Jewish Christian, found himself confronted with a God-fearing Roman centurion called Cornelius, the supposed evangelist was the one evangelised.[89] As we earth ourselves in our non-church culture we will discover how to become church among people with whom God is already actively engaged. But our discovery inevitably will necessitate changes of perception upon our part.[90]

Living Tradition or Dead Traditionalism?

Central to my response to what I've called 'Paul's missionary logic' is the recognition that the church's calling to be counter-cultural has to be matched by a recognition that it has to bed itself down in a new culture in order that it becomes aware of what God is already doing there, as well as be seen and heard

---

[89]   See Acts 10: 1 – 11: 18.
[90]   Part of the 'changes of perception' will involve our discovering the complexity of modern culture, made up as it is of many sub-cultures. If the church is to address modern culture effectively it will need to adopt different strategies appropriate to each sub-culture. We are not dealing with a society undergirded by a common meta-narrative. Indeed, it is arguable that our speaking of 'culture' is to misunderstand the nature of what we are speaking about. When used in this essay, therefore, the reader will want to note that the world 'culture' refers to a multi-cultural world of great diversity.

in ways that enable the gospel to be recognised. Church mission strategies must reflect both tasks, swinging from one to the other like a pendulum, embracing both equally. Let me finish by returning to Romans, where we find a typical church quarrel, inevitably one concerned with innovation. As faith-traditions develop changes happen to them. When are changes a faithful development of the living tradition? When are they not? We continually are asking such questions, whether it is about women in the church, styles of music in our worship, or even the church paintwork! In Rome, Jewish Christians were horrified by what the Gentile Christians had done to what they had passed on to them, meanwhile Gentile Christians found it difficult to equate some of the Jewish Christian's revered practices with the 'living tradition' – from their perspective they seemed more like 'the dead hand of traditionalism'. And every age of the church has had to face the task of distinguishing between 'a living tradition' and 'a deadly traditionalism'.

As is often the case, important distinctions are easier to formulate than to employ. As the Roman church example amply shows, what is 'living tradition' for some is 'deadly traditionalism' for others. That helps explain why change in the church is often accompanied by discord, and hence pain. It also is the reason why there ought to be a place for difference and variety in an inclusive church. Nevertheless, such observations and suggestions ought not deflect us from pressing home a very proper question: Are what we take to be unalterable 'givens' of the living tradition really 'unalterable', or do they actually manifest themselves as the barriers we erect to avoid the real gospel imperative to take risks in faith? I have noted over the years how we ministers of religion find it easier to ask that question of our church members than of ourselves! Be that as it may, ask it we *all* must: Is what I'm clinging on to for dear life really a given?   Would our moving on not be a help to those who are not yet part of us? We ought to remember that the only biblical model for change is 'death' followed by 'resurrection'!

The cultural gap between the church and Western society is far greater than most of us suppose or many of want to face up to. Those who try to bridge the gap from the church side will inevitably end up being accused by some of watering things down, not really understanding the tradition, and advocating change for change sake – precisely the kind of things Jewish Christians in Rome must have said about the Gentile church members. Church history shows how very difficult it is for an institutional church to live by the gospel it preaches: dying to itself in order to live to God for others. But as we face a radically new missionary situation, that is the difficulty and challenge we all have to face.

CHAPTER SIX

PENDULUM THEOLOGY

I am a theologian, but so is every Christian – even if those who are ordained do not usually place the word 'theologian' at the top of their CV's, and those who count themselves as 'lay' people may have been led by years of clerical domination to ignore that fact. Thinking critically and constructively about the Christian witness of faith is a responsibility that comes with the territory of being a Christian. We need to know what to say and why we are saying it, otherwise our witness will have no anchorage in tradition or relevance to contemporary issues or current debates; we need to know what to do and why we are doing it, otherwise our mission may end up being disconnected with the Christ event and lacking either a pastoral or prophetic cutting edge in society. By doing theology, Christians and churches maintain their identity and establish their credibility. It is an ongoing task.

Unlike most others in the church, however, I am a theologian by training and almost by profession. My mentors convinced me that I was called to help churches think theologically about their witness and mission. I was educated to make the best out of my theological abilities, and thinking theologically for and with the 'gathered saints' is what matters to me. Doing theology is part of my 'hinterland' – along with cricket, bird watching and classical music; it is the essential core of my Christian vocation. Being a theologian, however, has tended sometimes to make me somewhat marginal to both local and wider church life, not least because the critical function of being a theologian will invariably challenge the current ecclesial status quo. John Calvin, of course, found a place in his understanding of Christian ministry for 'teachers', alongside 'ministers', 'elders' and 'deacons'.[91] Perhaps I was born in the wrong age, an anti-intellectual milieu in which 'doing' has tended to overshadow 'thinking'? Be that as it may, I am what I am: a theologian!

Whatever we make of the contemporary predicament of the mainstream churches, underlying all our problems, as well as preventing us from grasping new possibilities, is the fact that, as individual Christians and churches, we are not theological enough. Lacking the critical edge which theology brings we are unable to untangle the living tradition from the thickets of deadly traditionalism; minus the constructive forces which theology opens up we miss out on discovering fresh ways and more credible expressions of the gospel. Hitherto, I have often tended to

---

[91]   John Calvin, *Institutes of the Christian Religion*, ed. John T. McNeill and tr. Ford Lewis Battles (Philadelphia: The Westminster Press, 1960), 4.3.4.

say that we do not think enough about what we say and do, but in fairness that is not true. At every level of the church, there is a lot of thinking going on. Indeed, some might say that we spend so much time thinking that we never get round to doing much! But the kind of critical and constructive thinking I understand as theology has not been central to many of our debates and discussions over the years. We have not been in the habit of assessing the adequacy of our life against the normative Jesus traditions in scripture, nor have we tested the credibility of our witness against contemporary canons of truth. Otherwise, we would have long since escaped from many of the habits which tie us down, have become less defensive about perceived orthodoxies and been opened up more to fresh expressions of Christian believing.

Theology is the process and product of critical reflection on Christian praxis.[92] It is critical since it asks and answers the question: Is what we are saying and doing in this or that piece of witness congruent with the Christian witness normed for us by the early Jesus traditions as well as credible given contemporary understandings of meaning and truth? Theology is also constructive since it raises and responds to the question: What is it that we are to say and do today in our Christian witness if we are to stand in a living relationship with the apostolic witness to Jesus and make sense, as well as a difference, in today's world. To do theology in this way, of course, involves being steeped in two cultures: the biblical culture, since it is only through the Bible that we can return to the foundational events of our religious tradition, and contemporary culture, given that it is only by knowing about it and being close to its heartbeat that we will be able to address it, engage with it and play our part in its life. Earlier, I explored this understanding of the nature and task of Christian theology in the context of Christian mission. The idea of 'pendulum theology' emerged.

The pendulum image has attracted a great deal of interest. It was picked up by Sheilagh Kesting, the theological reflector at the October 2005 meeting of Mission Council. As well as with the polar opposites of 'countercultural' and 'incultural', she found my image also working for other supposed alternatives in our discussions: 'local' and 'universal' in church polity, 'growth' and 'vulnerability' in mission, 'unity and 'diversity' in ecumenism. There are many more examples of course of the way seemingly contradictory opposites need a perspective which affirms our need to hold together both sides of a polarity. Given my view of theology this inevitably will be the case, since theology involves the interaction of two diverse cultures: Christian tradition and post-modern world, both of which, in their respective ways, are diverse and plural, and both of which are grounded in the creative and redeeming work of

---

[92]   See Schubert M. Ogden, *On Theology* (San Francisco: Harper & Row Publishers, 1986).

God. But to suggest that an authentically Christian praxis for the contemporary world is as incapable of being read off the Bible's pages as it is of being generated out of post-modern culture as a matter of course is to invite attack from both sides of the theological encounter between inherited tradition and contemporary worldview. Conservative Christians will accuse me of being unbiblical, while my more secularist friends outside the church will think I have succumbed to the irrational. But to what Bible are my Christian friends referring? Presumably one more unified and less diverse than the one I have to hand! And whose rationality are my non-church colleagues using when making their judgements? As a 'first-born' scientist and 'born again' theologian committed to integrate the worlds of religion and science, I find it heartening that whenever the brilliant Richard Dawkins steps up to attack religion equally brilliant intellectuals, some of them scientists, are on hand in religion's defence! No amount of empirically based reasoning could possibly prove or disprove the existence of God, who by definition is the ground of all things, and thereby logically odd by being of a different order, metaphysical and necessary rather than empirical and contingent – as the ancient ontological argument for God's existence points out. Both inside and outside the church, people seem incapable or unprepared to take into account the complexities involved in the Christian tradition's interaction with culture, in general, let alone contemporary culture, in particular. It is hard work being a theologian in a sound-byte culture, although my conversation partners keep me going!

One of these partners noted that as a pendulum swings, it creates friction and, hence, 'produces' energy. This reminds us, using a popular metaphor in current church discussions, that the wings of the church do not have to stand in opposition but actually can help us fly. I grew up experiencing two ways of conducting the quest for theological adequacy and the search for a credible Christian praxis: the winner takes all intellectual battle which sees one side defeat another and the drafting exercise which employs subtle hermeneutical dexterity to find a compromise which suits all sides. Both have a place, but so does a 'polar' or 'hybrid' or 'collage' approach which aims to synthesise rather than to defeat or to compromise. Nevertheless, we must recognise that a pendulum is not a windmill. There are some things at either end of the many theological spectra which we must not choose or simply cannot embrace, since they put us out of contact with the living tradition of faith normed by the apostolic witnesses to Jesus or simply are incredible to the contemporary mind. We also need to remember that a temptation to be relevant at all costs needs to be controlled by the fact that what our age counts as relevant may be neither congruent with the apostolic witness nor, upon close inspection, credible. Our ability to bypass the challenges of Jesus in favour of a comfortable piety is only matched by our seemingly endless capacity to chase novelty, follow fads or foster incredulity. On historical as well as theological grounds, 'popular' Christianity is somewhere between a dangerous illusion and an utter contradiction of terms.

Another conversation partner proved equally thought provoking. A good pendulum needs a strong spring to keep it going! We quickly agreed that there is a power behind, within and beyond the church that provides the momentum for the Christian project. We use words like 'grace', 'God' or 'Spirit' to describe it. But the Reformed tradition has a propensity to confuse that 'power', which sometimes is as breathtakingly humble as at other times awesomely mighty in holiness, with a book. We got into the habit way back in the sixteenth and seventeenth centuries of objecting to fellow Christians who were habitually confusing the 'power' (and also the 'presence' and 'promise' of course) with ministerial offices and orders in general and bishops and the papacy in particular. But all too easily Reformed churches found themselves enthroning a book at the same time they were trying to dethrone the Pope. The respective sides in the Reformation dispute both claimed that their particular authority was inspired, even though of course, both stand under the same 'norm beyond all norming', namely, the Word: the power, presence and promise of gracious Love which is at the very heart of the cosmos. To suggest otherwise is to court idolatry, though to be idolatrous waving a Bible may seem to Protestant eyes rather more virtuous than being observed asserting Papal infallibility. Theologically speaking, of course, both are formally *and* materially equally problematical.

I have been increasingly puzzled during my ministry why the United Reformed Church continues to claim that "the Word of God in the Old and New Testaments, discerned under the guidance of the Holy Spirit, is the supreme authority for the faith and conduct of all God's people" [93] when, in practice, most of our members never open their Bibles one week to the next. After a recent 'question and answer' session, a young woman tackled me for suggesting that a rediscovery of the Bible was one of the major prerequisites of the United Reformed Church ever being able to 'Catch the Vision'. Was it strategic, she asked, to place such emphasis upon a book that has been "oppressive to women, plainly wrong on many things and taken over by fanatics"? "Well", I responded, "it *is* a product of a bygone age – even if the first churches were more open to women than many later and some contemporary ones; it *is* 'plainly wrong on many things' – but then it was never meant to be a text-book; and hopefully, you'll realise I'm no fanatic!" The woman was not convinced, and no doubt she continues her spiritual searching around the religious pick and mix counters of our post-modern age. She had been led into a negative view about the

---

[93]   An affirmation required of all those who enter upon the designated ministries of the United Reformed Church: elder, minister and church-related community worker.

nature and purpose of the Bible through her observations of Christian use of it, and given the evidence around she might be affirmed in the stance she has taken. Any attempt to take her in a more positive direction, though, would have required the opportunities only an extended pastoral ministry provides. But are our churches the kind of places where it would be provided?

That young woman is not alone in thinking, for example, that the message of the Genesis I creation story is of the same logical order as the theory of evolution. *The Guardian* recently ran a story on the Archbishop of Canterbury with "Archbishop: stop teaching creationism. Williams backs science over Bible".[94] What Rowan Williams might have wanted to say, of course, is that biblical stories like Genesis I are 'myths', stories which convey deep metaphysical truths while not being empirically factual. Being just such a story, Genesis I conveys a host of penetrating insights into God's creative genius, even if the account viewed cosmologically is not factually accurate. But the Archbishop would not have dared use the word 'myth' because, as we all know, 'myth' in popular speech is a synonym for 'untruth'. What Williams actually said was as follows:

> I think creationism is, in a sense, a kind of category mistake, as if the Bible were a theory like any other theories. Whatever the biblical account of creation is, it's not a theory alongside theories. It's not as if the writer of Genesis or whatever sat down and said, 'Well, how am I going to explain all this . . . I know: In the beginning God created the heavens and the earth! So if creationism is presented as a stark alternative theory alongside other theories, I think there's just been a jarring of categories. It's not what it's about . . . My worry is creationism can end up reducing the doctrine of creation rather than enhancing it.[95]

The Archbishop is quite correct, but it takes someone with a background in mid-twentieth century linguistic philosophical debate to grasp fully what he means by a 'category mistake'!

On reflection, it is not at all surprising that a large number of thoughtful Christians live out their lives at some distance from the Bible. They belong to a culture dominated by empirical science and utilitarian description. If a claim cannot be 'measured' for accuracy, or shown to be of practical use, it is by-passed, and when propositions cannot be reduced to sound-bytes they are dismissed. But a great deal of what is truth, insightful and worthwhile is quite irreducible to these current demands. As long as we play 'the biblical game' according to the rules which govern the thinking of secularists

---

94   *The Guardian*, 21.03.06.
95   Ibid.

and fundamentalists alike, the Bible will be ignored by many of our more perceptive church members and remain the province of those the young woman described as 'fanatics'. The biblical genre seldom belongs, particularly when it really matters, to what our culture calls 'facts'. It operates with 'stories', 'myths', 'metaphors' and 'symbols' which take people into the 'beyond', both of their empirical understanding and towards proper obedience. The Bible teaches us that 'God: is "logically odd"[96] and misunderstood when treated on the same wavelength as electrons, tables or even persons. Scripture invites imagination from us as we 'play' with its literary forms to discover ways in which they work for us in our context and era, given that they may have worked differently for other people in different times and places.

In common with many colleagues in the Reformed tradition, my theology has been generated through preaching. A great deal of what I have read about preaching, as well as my performances as a preacher and that of others, seems to have been a major contributor to the way in which the Bible has become a closed book for many in our churches. Instead of opening up the biblical literature for our hearers, we preachers have in fact helped close it up for them. "This is what this story or passage means", I have said in effect, when what I should have been doing is taking the congregation on an adventure with the biblical text. The great exegetical temptations are seldom avoided: to answer a supposed question rather than question a supposed answer, to put it all down in a nutshell and forget that not all our hearers are nuts like us, or to become matter of fact when, really, the 'facts' which actually matter cannot be reduced to mere facts. 'Stories' need more stories to elucidate them; 'myths' demand exploration and interpreting not taking at face value; 'metaphors' need playing with endlessly until they break down upon the weight of application. We must allow the different genres of the biblical witness to make us fully sensual with truth: looking, listening and tasting our way into the adventure of the gospel, not just hearing it.

Whatever else being biblical involves, it certainly entails Reformed Christians reading the biblical texts imaginatively rather than one-dimensionally. The stories, myths and metaphors we find in those texts often had a life of their own before being pressed into use by the biblical writers. They will show their enduring worth today if we give them an opportunity to address us on their terms rather than ours. What is remarkable about the Bible is not how foreign it is to us, but how its varied literature constantly directs us to common human experiences from which we can construct our stories of faith ever anew.

---

[96]   See, for example, I.T. Ramsay's *Religious Language* (London: SCM Press, 1957) and *Models for Divine Activity* (London: SCM Press, 1973). Some of my very early theological explorations were greatly helped by this great churchman.

CHAPTER SEVEN

PLAYING WITH A METAPHOR

Inaccurate it may be, but the Authorised Version translation of Proverbs 29: 18 points to a profound truth: "Where there is no vision, the people perish".[97] Persons as well as peoples live on the basis of hopes they strive to actualise and utopias they try to establish in their time and place. We imagine how we would like things to be, and then we put things in place which hopefully will achieve the things for which we are aiming. The future we hope for therefore helps us construct our present world, with our dreams and visions, underpinned of course by necessary realism, thus helping make life creative and fulfilling. This is as true for us today as it was for those beleaguered Christians to whom the Seer of Patmos addressed the book of *Revelation*.

I say 'beleaguered' because when John wrote *Revelation* the Christian churches he was addressing were facing great persecution. Martyrdom was almost synonymous with being a Christian for many church members. What hope could be offered to people who were as likely as not going to perish on account of their faith? In seeking to answer that question John presented an amazingly provocative, yet symbolic, picture of the Eternal City, a newly redeemed and reconstructed world in which all present evils have been overcome and the faithful at last are at one with their creator. His language is sometimes as puzzling to the contemporary Western mind as it would have been transparent to its first audiences. This is partly due to the way we are not as steeped in the biblical imagery John uses as perhaps we were once, and partly due to our intellectual framework being less attuned to the world of 'myth', 'metaphor' and 'symbol'. We are somewhat held captive by the one dimensional literalism of mathematical calculation, statistical prediction and scientific fact. Hence, when understood on *our* terms and divorced from the thought-world with which the Seer of Patmos was operating, *Revelation* often remains at best a 'closed book' and at worst becomes the province of fanatics and sectarians. This is not literature to be read literally; it invites and indeed requires the use of our imagination.

In my thinking about the contemporary mission of the church I have been drawn to two particular features of John's apocalyptic vision. The first illustrates a basic presupposition of everything I believe about the church. In the Eternal City,

---

[97]　Cf., "Where there is no prophecy, the people cast off restraint" (NRSV) and "With no one in authority, the people throw off all restraint" (REB).

John tells us, there is no temple (Revelation 21: 22), the interface between church and society having been broken down in a surprisingly radical way. Our 'churchy' tendencies might have led us to expect the Eternal City to be one great temple, the final ark into which all the faithful are ultimately gathered. What John presents us with however is a world in which organised religion is no longer needed and the secular world has been perfected. In John's view, God's presence permeates the City's whole life, not just the fellowship of the Christian martyrs. Let this be a lesson to us: the church is always a temporal means to the eternal end of all things of worth and value to God being drawn into the divine fellowship. We are called, therefore, to be witnesses in the world of the all-embracing liberating work of God which has been focussed for Christians in Jesus and is experienced by us in ongoing and enduring ways through the Spirit. As sign and sacrament of that work the church has a missionary basis. We are that 'people's movement' within the world which testifies and displays God's promised alternative world, the new heaven and the new earth (Revelation 21: 1).

The church regrettably is ever prone to become trapped in an institution which serves its own ends. The people's movement called to be a sign, expression and anticipation of God's promised inclusive community invariably turns inward, seeking its meaning, purpose and destiny in its internal activities rather than its encounters with society. This brings us to the second feature of John's great vision I want to explore: the arrival of the Eternal City does not usher in the end of God's redeeming and sustaining activity. According to John, God is not just content to look after the eternal well-being of a handful of Christians; God is also concerned to draw into the divine fellowship the whole of humankind, with all the many peoples' varied cultural achievements. "People will bring into it the glory and the honour of the nations' (Revelation 21: 26). God's work, meanwhile, goes on beyond the City, irrigating the ground, maintaining the tree whose leaves are for "the healing of the nations" (Revelation 22: 2).

The existence of the river flowing out of the City, reminds us that, in John's view, God's liberating work is rather more expansive than Christians have sometimes supposed. John, of course, is tapping into a seam of rich biblical symbolism. In the second creation story, God gives life to the created order through the water which flows out of Eden to become the four great rives of the Ancient Near East. The metaphor of the river is thereby used to signify the way God sustains creation (Genesis 2: 10-14). The prophets also use it to point to 'salvation' [98] and 'prosperity'.[99] When the writer of *Revelation* draws upon the metaphor however

[98]   See Isaiah 43: 19, 20.
[99]   See Isaiah 66: 12.

it is most likely that he is echoing Ezekiel's use as a hope for food and purification: ". . . everything will live where the river goes" (Ezekiel 47: 9). The message is clear: God's work will only come to an end when all things have been 'refreshed', and since the Christian church is called to be a sign and sacrament of that 'refreshment' the metaphor of the 'river' can help us remember important things about being church.

Rather than trade in abstractions, let us look at a real river and reflect theologically upon its major features. As we journey along it, we will notice things of importance about God's work and hence the true calling of the church. We will be 'playing' with a metaphor and discovering that the church is faithful when we gather around, join in and promote what God is already doing. The river is already flowing; the church's job is to jump in it, or travel on it, and, most certainly, go with the flow! The river I am choosing to use as our living metaphor is the one I grew up alongside, the Aire.

The Aire begins above Malham in the Yorkshire Dales, heads south-east through the industrial landscape of West Yorkshire before flowing into the Ouse, which in turn enters the Humber estuary and hence the North Sea. If we were to take a helicopter flight over the Aire's entire length, we would notice tremendous topographical changes and the river's changing moods. The first insight that emerges from our playing with the 'river' metaphor concerns the way which the work of God changes from time to place, thereby necessitating that our Christian response to God's ongoing work needs shaping in contextually appropriate ways. There is no way of being church that is independent of time and place, just as all rivers are different at their various stages. At one point the Aire is little more that a trickling stream, at another it is fast-flowing water. We can speculate about the kind of water in which the church today finds herself. Our era is one of rapid social change, a world which Thomas Hawkins has likened to being "a permanent white-water society",[100] so we need perhaps to turn to those who know something about white-water if we are to learn appropriately from our metaphor.

Canoeists will warn us against doing nothing or doing too much in rapid white-water. We should use our paddles to guide us at speed through the water. In our current climate it is difficult in the whirlwind of change to separate out the spirit of God from the spirit of the age. It is as futile simply always to go with the flow as it is to resist all change as a matter of principle. Either way leads to destruction. Consequently, we must steer a course avoiding hazards but still moving ahead, affirming whatever we can of the age – ". . . whatever is true, whatever is

---

[100]   Thomas R. Hawkins, *The Learning Congregation: A New Vision of Leadership* (Louisville, Kentucky: Westminster John Knox Press, 1997), p3. Hawkins is quoting Peter B. Vaill.

honourable, whatever is just, whatever is pure, whatever is pleasing, whatever is commendable" (Philippians 4: 8). Somehow we have to hold on to the belief that God is in all this with us, even if in an important sense also beyond it all.

Even briefly to mention the rocks brings us to our second insight: not everything can be affirmed and quite often we are responsible for the resistance to God's purposes. We have now left the helicopter to stand beside the Aire at Castleford. Here the river is quite wide after it has flowed through the industrial heartlands. When I was a boy the woollen industry was thriving and the Aire was an orange sterile soup at this point due to the effluent from the dye-works and wool-processing factories up stream. The river is much cleaner these days, partly due to there being less industry around and partly the result of our greater environmental awareness. But we all know of the countless ways in which we 'pollute' God's ongoing work and thwart Love's purposes. Our additions to the river are not always beneficial, so we often stand in need of forgiveness, with penitence being humankind's only fitting disposition. As we now look out at a river which once again supports life when once it only harboured death, we are reminded that not all is lost. The world has seen the divine forgiveness focussed in the Christ event, so we must always believe that there can be new life. The river need not always be choked by our pollution; through God's grace we can work to see it live again.

Enough though of the one-time seedier parts of the Aire, let us go to the river's starting point for our third insight. Just where the Aire begins has been a source of confusion. Dales' folk long ago would have taken us into the breath-taking scenery of Malham Cove in search of the Aire's source. This is the home of dipper and grey wagtail, a beautiful, gentle stream along which kingfishers' dart, leading to awesome limestone cliffs upon which peregrines nest – these days in front of an inquisitive holidaying public via the RSPB telescopes annually focussed upon them. Having taken us to the face of the cliffs, the old-timers would have looked down at the bubbling water emerging beneath them and declared this point to be the birth of their Yorkshire river. It may have inspired Charles Kingsley's *The Water Babies*, but it isn't the source of the Aire! To find the source we have to take an invigorating walk up to the top of the Cove, over the grikes in the limestone pavement, and then on to Malham Tarn, because as geologists and geographers discovered the southern outlet of the Tarn is the true starting point of the Aire. What happens is that the newly-born river sinks underneath the limestone close by the Tarn and then re-appears at Aire Head Springs beyond Malham itself. The sub-terranean tendencies of the Aire confused folk for generations, and so it is with God: the divine life-giving generosity is not always observable, nor is it always traceable to the expected places. Obediently, the true church has sometimes had to go underground, leaving the false church visible on the surface. When Bonhoeffer and his prison comrades gathered under Word and around a makeshift Table, Christ was in their midst, even if others in more visible and well-attended churches assumed Christ's presence was with them. Today, as some of the traditionalist congregations of contemporary mainstream churches wither and die, new patterns of faithfulness and ways of being church are springing up beyond the mainstream. We must never under-estimate the subterranean tendencies of the living God!

It is so invigorating at Malham Tarn that on a tranquil day it is a place to linger and enjoy. On such days, the water of the newly established river seems pure and clear, although you should always take note of what the Swaledale sheep are doing further up-stream! Come winter however, and particularly when the snow is melting, the Aire's water will be coloured by peat collected as the water moves over the soggy ground. This brings us to our fourth insight: just as Pennine rivers are seldom the clearest at their sources, so the earliest examples of the church are not necessarily the ones for us to model. I can understand the motivation of those Christians who want to model the contemporary church on some pure biblical example of the church. After all, the Protestant emphasis upon the authority of scripture drives us in that direction. But the project is doomed from the start: no 'pure' church is recorded in scripture. Biblical churches, like our churches, are places in which wheat and tares grow until the harvest. And, in any case, our particular context requires a model of church suitable for the twenty first century, post-modern West, not the first century Ancient Near East. We have to find patterns of obedience suitable for our age, just as the first Christians had to do for there time. Sometimes we will see fit to repeat what they did; at other times we will need to adapt what they said and did to fit our era; yet other crucial times necessitate that we plough fresh furrows. Living in the Christian tradition involves fresh ownership and innovation, just as much as it also sometimes means repeating what has been handed on. Finding out how all this works out for us today is a great challenge, but it is not a greater challenge than the one which faced earlier generations.

Appropriately, we find our fifth insight as we conclude our exploration of the 'river' metaphor by visiting the end of the Air, as it flows into the Ouse, then into the Humber Estuary and the great North Sea. We haven't had time to reflect on the significance of the many steams and tributaries which flow in and out of the Aire; nor have we had time to consider the significance of waterfalls – such things can be left to the imaginative reader! At the end, in the North Sea, diverse rivers have come together in unity, with a resulting abundance of life that no one river could ever sustain. Our metaphor consequently throws up a model for ecumenism. But if we follow the vision of the Seer of Patmos this will involve more than the coming together of churches, or even religions. John's vision is of a gathering of *everything* in the cosmos in fellowship with God. That, needless to say, is the vision and goal to which the church must aspire as we explore ways which make God's universal love and forgiveness real for everyone.

PART THREE

REFLECTIONS AND RESOURCES

CHAPTER EIGHT

TEN OBSERVATIONS BY WAY OF 'THANK YOU'

My year as Moderator of General Assembly is now over. It has been an exiting and stimulating year which has brought me hitherto undreamt of opportunities and a great deal of personal affirmation. Carrying out my duties and responsibilities became a major factor in my recovery from serious illness, with United Reformed Church hospitality and kindnesses helping me gain strength and energy – and, perhaps, too much weight! I would like to thank all who made the year possible: the Yorkshire Synod who nominated me, the Assembly who elected me, Krystyna who looked after my diary and travel arrangements and Pat who shared it all with me. *Reform's* many readers will have read about my travels and what I have got up to, while this book is a record of what I have felt called to say to the United Reformed Church during my year of office.

As the curtain comes down on their Moderatorial year, Moderators are given a final opportunity to address Assembly. It provides us with an opening to speak about the church as we have found it. Having noted the kind of occasions to which I was invited, I can only say that Moderators run the risk of drawing conclusions about the local church scene from somewhat untypical experiences. We visit Districts and, hence, attend many regional meetings and united events. Only twenty-five per cent of my activity has taken in local churches, and very often those visits were associated with anniversary celebrations with their inflated attendances. It quickly became clear to me that my fifteen years as, first, Tutor and, then, Principal of Northern College had provided me with an overview of the church far more in keeping with reality than the picture with which I was been given as Moderator. Far from being an ivory tower, aloof from the cut and thrust of local church life, that particular seat of theological education and training was kept in touch with the way things actually are in our churches by our students who were all on church placements throughout their time with us. And there is a book to be written on what I heard about the saintliness and the sinfulness which typifies our congregations!

Given the information I gleaned from those ecclesiastical 'spies', as well as what I picked up as an itinerant preacher, it is a matter of report rather than a show of arrogance when I say that, during the past year, I have learned very little

about the United Reformed Church that I did not already know. But the 'very little'
is significant, and I will turn to it first before moving on to areas that my recent
experience have merely confirmed. It comes in three observations:

(i)   **The churches are able to exercise a remarkable degree of influence
        on national politics.**

I have hitherto under-emphasised the extent to which the secularization
hypothesis penetrated my assumptions as I wrestled with it almost forty years ago.
While I have never been in agreement with the 'Christ against culture' views of the
likes of Lesslie Newbigin, I had not recognized the extent to which I had assumed
that, somehow, the political powers were a threat to the Christian vision. After the
Cenotaph ceremony the opportunity to lobby politicians who were very interested
in the church's view of things was greater than I had been led to believe, or had
bargained for. It turned out to be a lost opportunity due to a failure on my part to
use the chance well. Alongside this, we witnessed during the year the extent of the
church's influence on the Government in the substantial changes 'we' managed to
generate in the prospective legislation concerning gambling and blasphemy. When
we work ecumenically 'on' the Government we have more influence than we think.
The churches represent a huge pressure group. In a multi-faith society whose
many voices the legislators need to 'hear', we usually under-estimate our influence.
Paradoxically as the era of Christendom recedes, Governments of all party hues find
an increasing need to hear the views of the faith-communities.

(ii)   **The United Reformed Church has not been very good at projecting
        the significance of Reformed insights and practices in a way
        which does justice to our important position on the worldwide
        ecumenical stage.**

Perhaps our ecumenical commitment has made us reticent to promote
Reformed policy and practice? Perhaps the fact that we have the Church of England
as our 'big brother' hides from us a recognition that, in a wider European context,
the natural conversation partner with Rome and Orthoxody is Geneva and not
Canterbury? At a time when the Elizabethan Settlement is far from settled, and
many within Anglicanism expect their communion to cleave apart, there are reasons
to be far from shy about our traditions of inclusivity, our objections to episcopacy,
our patterns of conciliarity, our unease about Establishment, our ongoing belief in a
'learned ministry' and our commitment to a lay-ministry focussed in the Eldership.
We have insights to offer and our being in a minority does not make them irrelevant.
Many United Reformed Church people report that Reformed 'habits' and convictions

get lost in some of our local ecumenical arrangements. Our integrity is sometimes in danger of becoming submerged under a commendable desire to accommodate. This concern however needs placing alongside and in tension with my third piece of new learning.

(iii) **During the life-time of the United Reformed Church ecumenical activity has developed and increased, although not in the ways some of us expected or hoped.**

I was among those who expected the United Reformed Church to become a catalyst for further organic church union in Britain and therefore to have a very short shelf-life. Some interpret the fact that this has not taken place as at least a disappointment if not quite a total failure, while others ring their hands at having arrived at what they see as an ecumenical *cul-de-sac*. During the year, Philip Morgan died. He was as passionate about church unity as many of the other early leaders of our small church. In an obituary for Philip, Jean Mayland remarked that "if the moribund ecumenical life of the British churches is to be revived, it needs a man or woman of Morgan's energy and vision to bring it about".[101] The phrase 'the moribund ecumenical life of the British churches' started me wondering about how such a claim could be substantiated given the large numbers of thriving ecumenical arrangements I was encountering on my travels.[102] Viewed from the perspective of a mid-twentieth century modernist blue-print for ecumenical engagement the life-time of the United Reformed Church has been ecumenically depressing. But what if that blue-print was fatally-flawed? What if, even, the passage of recent church history, with the world-wide growth of vibrant grass-roots ways of being church and the mushrooming of local ecumenical arrangements and post-denominational churches, is God's way of telling us, Rome notwithstanding, that ecclesiology works best 'bottom-up' rather than 'top-down'? 'Post-modern' messiness is proving more viable than 'modernist' neatness. This is hardly surprising given that the contemporary challenge is to be ecumenical in ways that are appropriate to a present culture which of course is rather different to the culture which shaped the visionary ecumenical thinking of our earlier pioneers. There is a way of reading our past which concludes that the life-time of the United Reformed Church has been a period of extremely lively and surprisingly creative ecumenism.

---

[101]   *The Guardian*, 03.11.2005.

[102]   Similar sentiments are found in Keith Forecast's review of Tony Tucker's *Reforming Ministry: Traditions of Ministry and Ordination in the United Reformed Church*. Tony's book reminds Keith of "ecumenical failure after failure" and prompts his wish that "we could aspire again to that glorious aim embedded with the United Reformed Church's Basis of Union" concerning visible unity. See *The Journal of the United Reformed Church History Society*, 7, 4 (May 2004) pp 281-281.

So much then for new areas of learning, but what of those things I have had confirmed during my year as Assembly Moderator? Seven areas are worthy of report.

(1) **Many of our churches are in terminal decline.**

A lot of congregations are struggling to keep going. Some have lost a sense of purpose; others have been deprived of their catchment areas due to population movement; quite a few would appear to have served their time and place well, but now that the world has moved on they are left without life. Given the age-profile of our congregations it seems inevitable that, without a miraculous revival, many of them will not be around in ten year's time. In some geographical areas and in certain congregations the rate of numerical decline is well above the national average. It is very difficult to see how a diminishing number of members can maintain the institution of which they are part, nationally and regionally as well as locally, if present trends continue, while it is tragic in some places to see faithful outcroppings of God's gathered saints being crushed by the weight of the institutional church they have inherited. Equally worrying is the way in which so many of our churches do not offer the quality of worship and pattern of congregational life to which many of us would want to become committed. In a competitive church market-place and within a non-denominational church culture, there are better alternatives on offer.

(2) **We find it easier to maintain dying churches than to create and resource new Christian causes.**

There is an ongoing conflict between the local congregation's demand for their slice of ministry and our wider calling to provide leadership in fresh areas of mission. Recent attempts to increase the number of Special Category Ministries is a step in the right direction, although it will need a lot of local and regional resource sharing if a real difference is to be made. Vast amounts of assets are frozen in church buildings which continue in village, town and city to play their part in the church 'over-provision' which since Victorian times has been so much a feature of our ecclesiastical landscape. Huge amounts of money cannot legally be used for anything other than maintaining church plant. It is painful to be reminded that Jesus invested in twelve disciples rather than the fabric of the temple or synagogue. We always seem able to find money for our buildings, even though we moan endlessly about the level of our financial commitments to the wider church. The Assembly can announce loudly that 'maintenance of the ministry' is the first charge on the local church, but we all know the local realities.

(3) **There is a conflict between, on the one hand, denominational requirements and expectations, and, on the other hand, what local churches want.**

'We' basically do not trust 'them', while in turn, 'they' get rather exasperated about 'us'. And some of 'them' and 'us' have the dexterity to change roles to suit the church councils in which we happen to be sitting! The wider contemporary culture of individualism runs throughout the church. It fits all too easily with those traditions of rugged Independency from which the conciliar structures of the United Reformed Church were hopefully going to set some of us free. Classic Independency of course provided the ecclesial shape which helped bankroll and energise Nonconformity's advance, but it comes to grief when we have to make painful adjustments to manage decline and try to create fresh starting points for growth. The conciliar dream of 1972 is now under acute pressure, as Assembly ever hopefully seeks to hold together the manifold aspirations of its thirteen synod fiefdoms, and local churches 'opt out' of denominational affairs or insist on keeping going when they are already dead. What kind of Assembly-driven strategy can there be when so much power and so many resources are vested in regional and local hands? We are part of a society which is suspicious of authority and reacts with hostility to centralised governance and unnecessary bureaucracy. If 'Catch the Vision' is to succeed it will have to be directed in such a way that the local church is enthused and enabled. No amount of structural alteration or agonising over national budgets will matter unless it all serves the primary interface of Christian mission, the local church's encounter with its neighbourhood and the wider community. I have heard many people saying that, given 'Catch the Vision's' starting point in structures and finance, they are sceptical about its outcome, even though they still wait in hope!

(4) **We are a diverse church.**

Our diversity contributes to the richness of the United Reformed Church at the same time as it threatens our overall cohesion and unity. We are ecclesiologically diverse, not just as a result of being a union of three church traditions but also because we are now found in an array of different and sometimes confusing shapes which typify the post-modern church scene. Different ways of being church these days reflect intra-as well as inter-denominational variations. It follows that we are a theologically diverse church. Different views are present in those many congregations which are clear expressions of locally grounded visible unity. The old denominational fault-lines labelled 'Congregational', 'Presbyterian' and 'Churches of Christ' have largely disappeared. We are also culturally diverse, being a church of three countries and one in which our multi-cultural congregations are among our most vibrant. Meanwhile, the wealth of our churches corresponds to the areas in which they are set: in the richer South or the poorer North, leafy richer suburb or poorer inner city. Amidst all this diversity it is sometimes difficult to hold the church together. This contemporary ecclesial phenomenon, of course, is not unique to the United Reformed Church.

(5)   **The most exciting things in our church life centre upon individuals and communities who are largely indifferent to 'run of the mill' denominational activities.**

Ground-breaking adventures in mission and ministry usually centre upon charismatic and prophetic individuals who often have to achieve their goals against the grain of church policy and with meagre financial resources. It is a pity that they sometimes encounter conciliar structures as 'no can do' bodies, but it is amazing how many find ways of managing them, overcoming them or even strategically avoiding them. As we seek to come to grips with our rapidly changing church scene we have to learn how to build the church around its spirit-filled people. The more rigid our church institution, the greater will become the present crisis in the church. We need flexibility and adaptability to go where life is – and life is always where there are Christians who are alive!

(6)   **The United Reformed Church has some impressive ministers who are doing some amazingly faithful and farsighted things.**

Not all of them, I hasten to add, were prepared for their ministries in Manchester, but some of them were! I worry however about our most gifted ministers having the stuffing knocked out of them by nonsensical deployment policies and deathly churches. I also worry about the twenty per cent or so of our ministers who are burnt out after faithful service, or who are no longer physically up to the job, or who are simply out of their depth. They do not have the benefit of belonging to an organisation which has an early retirement policy that serves as an aid to maintaining the quality of the organisation's delivery at the same time as looking after its failing and ailing employees.

(7)   **The fundamental task of the church remains essentially the same in every generation: it is all about gathered saints living out and delivering that Christian way of thinking, being and doing which is, at one and the same time, congruent with the inherited living tradition of faith as well as credible in our contemporary culture.**

The church's mission follows from faithful living at the interface between tradition and context. It can only be grasped and then shaped by those who know, in the bottom of their hearts as well as from the tops of their heads, that in Jesus Christ they have been made different, and those who then find themselves spiritually led and politically motivated to make a difference in their contemporary context. Because this is so I can report unequivocally that the primary issues we face from top to bottom concern neither structures nor resources. Our root problems are 'spiritual' and 'theological'; they invite serious questions about many of our current priorities, as individuals, as congregations, and as a denomination.

THE DELEGATION MODEL

Delegation is recognized as a key skill in business, in accepting broader responsibility and empowering others by supporting their development. Here delegation has been used as a model to help us reflect on God's relationship with us and on our relationship with God. God is cast as the ultimate delegater in order to help us explore what it means for us to be called by God, as partners in creation.

On the first day of creation, God made light – it felt exciting, so God called it day. Then God made darkness – it felt restful, so God called it night.

God smiled. Evening passed and morning came. And that's how the first day went by.

On the second day, God made the earth - God made the heavens above, and the earth beneath our feet. God made fire, and watched it dance. God made earth, and smelt its freshness. God made water, and drank it down.

God smiled. Evening passed and morning came. And that's how the second day went by.

On the third day, God made plants. Some God made to be intricate and delicate. Some God made to be useful and others God made, just for fun.

God smiled. Evening passed and morning came. And that's how the third day went by.

On the fourth day, God made the sun to appear by day, and the moon to put in an appearance by night. And just for that touch of extra sparkle, God made the stars, and was delighted by them.

God smiled. Evening passed and morning came. And that's how the fourth day went by.

On the fifth day, God made birds for the skies and fish for the seas. God got out a paint brush and painted stripes and spots, feathers and scales, in every colour and style imaginable.

God smiled. Evening passed and morning came. And that's how the fifth day went by.

In the evening, God was exhausted by the number of things going on at the same time. The Spirit was in her basket, tired from all the running around. She was limiting her movements to wistful twitches of the eyebrows and a very occasional flick of her tail. So God thought about this for a while, and decided to refer to a management hand book.

After some reflection, God concluded that it was easy to start large initiatives, but not so easy to sustain them. The best idea it seemed … was delegation … achieving results through others and freeing time to concentrate on new priorities. Delegation. But to whom?

On the sixth day, God made animals of every shape and size imaginable. God also wanted someone to talk to and to share the work with, and so God created human beings. God asked the human beings to look after the earth, the skies, the seas, the animals and plants, and all the resources within them.

God smiled. Evening passed and morning came. And that's how the sixth day went by.

By the seventh day, God stopped working, curled up on the couch and had a nice big mug of hot chocolate. But by mid afternoon, God began to feel uneasy – was this delegation idea actually working?

God looked at the management handbook again, this time more closely. God got out a flip chart and pen and started to write down the five commandments of delegation.

1   Provide complete information on Company Policy, communicating the values and behaviours with which the task should be undertaken.

2   Delegate all types of task – not just the trivial, boring or unimportant. Make sure you are available to support your staff in their delegated tasks.

3   Delegation is a development opportunity for both you and your staff. Do not provide the answers, but help the person find them.

4   Delegate as widely and freely as possible (across boundaries etc).

5   Do not be hasty in criticising mistakes, and accept responsibility for all decisions in your department.

Hmm, thought God. Each one of those is worth reflecting on in turn.

And so, reaching for the diary, God marked out five windows of opportunity over the next few days to think them through…

Jill Thornton

HYMN

Based upon Isaiah 43: 15-21 and Acts 2: 38-47

God, our Creator, Source of truth and justice,
stride though earth's storms until all terrors cease;
defeat our warlike ways, our pride in battle,
brute force and cruelty that still increase:
sweep them aside in your relentless passion,
through steadfast love bring in your reign of peace.

Forbid our futile dwelling on past glories
and morbid gloom regarding present days.
Come, where our faith and hope are dry and barren,
to show us living springs in desert ways:
love's endless source of deeply flowing rivers,
quenching our thirst, inspiring us to praise.

Called to repent of doubt and disillusion,
we turn again to you, Christ crucified,
now resurrected, giving us your Spirit,
with hope and joy to take life in our stride:
the promise is for us and children's children,
and all whom God will call from far and wide.

So, God of life, and new life, keep us faithful,
renew the Church and make us worthy heirs
of the apostles, building on their teaching,
still breaking bread, in joyful hope that shares
faith's fellowship of love which, overflowing,
will bring earth peace, fulfilling all our prayers.

Alan Gaunt © 2005
Reproduced by permission of Stainer & Bell Ltd.
Rejoice and Sing 108

TUNE: *Som Stranden*

ACKNOWLEDGEMENTS

All biblical quotations are taken from the New Revised Standard Version of the Bible © 1989 & 1995 Division of Christian Education of the National Council of Churches in the United States

Page 10   'Let the Spirit Live' by Jonathon Porritt appeared in
           The Green Fuse © Schumaker Society   (permission sought)

           Dennis Potter in an interview with Mervyn Bragg
           © 1994 London Weekend Television
           (permission sought)

Page 26   Quotation from *Honest Religion for Secular Man*
           by Lesslie Newbigin;   SCM Press London 1966 used by permission
Page 30   Stanza from *Sing One and All a Song of Celebration*
           by Fred Pratt Green. Used by permission of Stainer & Bell

Page 42   Quotation from *The MacDonaldization of the Church* by John Drane.
           Used by permission of Darton Longman and Todd

Page 80   Quotation from *Transforming Mission* by David Bosch,
           Orbis Books, Maryknoll USA. Used by permission

Page 87   Michael Paul Gallagher in *The Tablet* 10th September 2005.
           Used by permission

Page 103   Article in *The Guardian* 21 March 2006. © Guardian Newspapers Ltd.
           Used by permission

Page 122   *God our Creator, Source of truth and justice*
           by Alan Gaunt. Used by permission of Stainer & Bell

Printed in the United Kingdom
by Lightning Source UK Ltd.
112626UKS00001B/358-405